This workbook is packed full of thought-provoking lists, helpful suggestions and lifesaving promises, all written in a clear, blunt and contemporary language that my teens really responded to. It is an excellent resource that will open the lines of communication between depressed teenagers and their loved ones. The author has turned personal tragedy and overwhelming parental challenges into a tool that I am confident will save lives.

Janet G.
-mother of one teenager with severe depression and two with bipolar illness

I'm Not Crazy

A WORKBOOK FOR TEENS WITH DEPRESSION AND BIPOLAR DISORDER

Linda de Sosa

IUNIVERSE, INC.
NEW YORK   BLOOMINGTON

I'm Not Crazy
A workbook for teens with depression and bipolar disorder

iUniverse books may be ordered through booksellers or by contacting:

iUniverse
1663 Liberty Drive
Bloomington, IN 47403
www.iuniverse.com
1-800-Authors (1-800-288-4677)

Because of the dynamic nature of the Internet, any Web addresses or links contained in this book may have changed since publication and may no longer be valid.

ISBN: 978-0-595-52118-0 (sc)
ISBN: 978-0-595-62182-8 (ebk)

Printed in the United States of America

iUniverse rev. date: 8/5/2009

I'M NOT CRAZY!!!

If someone who loves or cares for you has given you this book, they don't think you're crazy. However, they might think you are battling a disease called depression or bipolar depression. Hopefully, this book will help you understand your illness and help you cope. At the end of the workbook though, you have a choice. It isn't fair that you are sick. But, lots of people have illnesses like cancer that will kill them...soon. They don't have a choice. You do. You can decide that you want to seize life and offer it as much as you have. Or you can blame others or not reach out for help. No one can promise you it will be easy. But whoever gave you this book wants you around … and I bet you can find a lot of others out there who feel the same way.

Please give the following paragraph to your parents to complete:

Acceptance from parents
I love you, _____. I will always support you even though I may not approve of your actions. I especially value your_____. I want to see you grow old and be whatever is important to you. Love,_____

About the author:

When I turned 36, I suddenly became suicidally depressed. My mind constantly urged my body to kill itself over and over. During my months of hospitalization and therapy, I learned a lot about myself and my illness. I also met the love of my life and my soul mate, Brad. We were to marry, but he was living with demons of his own. He was alcoholic and bipolar which was combined with strong post traumatic stress disorder (PTSD) where he relived the war in Vietnam every day and night. We connected at every level, and I understood him through to his soul. However, he could not live with the intense pain any longer and took his own life. Thus, I became unique - someone who understands both sides of suicide victims.

Knowing him allowed me to recognize my own son as bipolar at 12 though no one believed me. Through years of supporting him, I learned a lot. He is now a successful college graduate. I thought we were in the clear. Then, on Christmas morning, 2009, my 28 year old son, Michael, succumbed to the demons of his depression and jumped off an overpass. He updated his Facebook status that "it was a long time coming and not to blame yourselves" from the top of the bridge. Of the hundreds that mourned him, only 3 knew he was depressed. None knew how seriously. Mental illness is just that, an illness, not a weakness. The strong are the ones who ask for help. I hope others can learn from my family so no one need go through this pain again. Please.

I am not clinically trained and don't pretend to be. I do have a BA in psychology, an MBA from Stanford, and a PhD in the School of Hard Knocks. I have read a lot of books and talked with a lot of people in my search for knowledge. **HOWEVER, it is most important that you involve medical professionals as you battle this illness**!

Linda de Sosa, 2010

FOREWARD

Linda de Sosa's workbook, "I'm Not Crazy" is an excellent new addition to the field of adolescent mental health treatment. Drawing from her own painful experience, she has created an excellent tool for helping teens successfully navigate the often turbulent adolescent years. Although not a licensed therapist, her research and insight is evident as her workbook is both highly professional and clinically accurate. Her abundant knowledge and compassion combine for a highly sensitive workbook that truly speaks to teens.

As a psychotherapist working with adolescents and their families, I have rarely seen a workbook that encompasses such a broad range of issues associated with adolescent mood disorders. As teens often have great difficulty identifying and articulating their thoughts and feelings, this workbook provides a vehicle for exploring their inner worlds. Utilizing "I Am Not Crazy" in a clinical setting provides a stimulus for meaningful dialogue and increased insights for clients. Many of the exercises are designed to increase cognitive and behavioral modifications that would result in a more positive, stable mood. Appropriate use of medication is also addressed.

Written for teens, it is both humorous and easy to read. I highly recommend it to therapists who are dedicated to facilitating a healing experience for adolescents struggling with a mood disorder.

Carol Cash, LMSW
Psychotherapist

Dedicated in loving memory of Michael and Brad - I'm spreading the word and helping others to honor you. Please stand behind me and support me with your love from above. And to my 3 other children, Tim, Bobby, and Alex – I love you.

The Warrior and the Child
By Linda de Sosa

Trapped in a body
Together
The warrior and the child.
The warrior takes the body to the edge
Again and again
To avenge the hurting child.
The child just hurts and feels and loves
And waits to be loved.
The warrior builds wall after wall
Again and again
To protect the innocent child.
The child just hides and cries and loves
And waits to be loved.
But behind the walls no one can see the child
To love the child
So the child receives no love from others
So the child receives no love from himself.
And when another soul finally reaches
Through the walls to the hurting child
And loves,
The warrior can't stop the child
From feeling and loving.
And now the child has gained the strength
To protect others from the warrior.
And as the child pushes the warrior
Over the edge
To destroy it forever,
He cries
Because they are trapped in a body
Together.

As I go through each day, I find myself constantly thinking and wondering. My mind is always wandering. It seems my mind has become more acute since I started dealing with my feelings. Grant you, I have a long way to go, and it sure as hell is not easy. Sometimes I feel like a scared little boy, and other times superhuman. Boy, what a strange mix. It is hard enough to let these things surface but to cope with them - well that is a whole new ballgame. Well, I'm determined to take a stand, for I'm used to being in the trenches and having my back up against the wall. For I know I will survive and get a firm grip on my life. No more attempts on my life. I will have victory over this - or at least peace. {Note from Brad's letters}

"It's been a long time coming – don't blame yourself"
and "I love you"
Michael's final texts and Facebook entry from the top
of the 10 story overpass before he jumped.

Contents

What is depression?

Overview

Let's talk about depression.

Name some sicknesses that make people sick for a week or less.

_____

What about a year or more?

_____
_____

Depression and bipolar depression are more like the second group.

Drawing by Clara Germiller, 15

If your school football team loses a game, some people might say, "I'm so depressed that we lost." That is not depression, the illness - that is sadness about something that happened. If your pet dies, you might be sadder for a longer time, but that's still not depression because you have a reason to be sad.

What has made your parents sad in the last month?

_____

What has made you sad? Write down 5 events and put them on the scale below.

A little sad   _____
More sad   _____
Saddest event _____

This sadness is a normal part of life. It is an emotion. Here are some other emotions. Write down an experience that made you feel:
Happy _____
Disappointed_____
Angry_____
Frustrated_____
Jubilant_____
Embarrassed_____

When was the last time you felt some of those?_____

Also, as a teenager, a lot of things conspire to make you **moody** naturally. Your hormones are raging; you don't recognize your body because of all the changes. Also, you have a lot of pressure in high school and who knows what you will do after graduation?

Depression is different than sadness or moodiness. It is a physical illness like a cold or diabetes. It is kind of hard to understand, but let's try.

Every thought you have is actually a little chemical reaction in your brain. A chemical called a neurotransmitter travels from neuron to neuron, crossing over synapses (empty spaces). The names of some of the neurotransmitters that you might hear about are dopamine, serotonin, and norepinephrine.

"I want to   Neuro   ➢ Neuron ➢ Synapse ➢ Neuron
go to bed"   Transmitter

"I like her"   Neuro   ➢ Neuron ➢ Synapse ➢ Neuron
                Transmitter

If you think about it (oh, there goes another neurotransmitter on the journey), it is a bit like a vitamin in our bloodstream.

Vitamin ➢ Blood ➢ Heart ➢ Lungs ➢ Other Organs

Sometimes, something blocks the flow. If something blocks the vitamin, we do not get needed nutrients. If something blocks the insulin in a diabetic, then they can go into a coma. If something stops the flow in our brain, then our thoughts become strange.

"I have a   Neuro   ➢ Neuron ➢ Synapse ≠ Neuron
good future" Transmitter   Floating in synapse &
                         sucked back into the neuron

The result becomes a black void, a nothingness. It is not sadness because that is an emotion. This is more like no emotions at all. Draw a picture of what you think a black hole might look like. That void is like depression.

Sometimes, a chemical gets stuck in the "on" position, which creates "intrusive thinking" or the same thought over and over and over and over and over and over.....

And sometimes, the brain will go down into the nothingness and then swing back like a pendulum and all your thoughts start racing and nothing can stop them and you are hyper and excited and just keep going and going like the famous pink bunny until you go back down again... This is called bipolar depression or manic depression.

Medication can help with all of these – that's the good news. But you have to admit you are sick and that you need the medicine. And you have to take it – the right amount -when it is time to take it every day. When you are hungry, you feed yourself, right? Well, when the doctor told you what medications to take when, he or she knew that your brain would be hungry for them at that time. So feed your brain!!

MEDICATION

Taking medicine makes me feel:_____

If you don't feel like taking meds, **you're not alone**. The major reasons why people don't take their meds:
1) It's fun to be manic
2) Don't know they need them
3) Side effects (imagined or real)
4) Denial that anything is wrong
5) Too depressed to take them
6) Fear of becoming dependent of them
7) The bottles and TV commercials say that they might increase the possibility of suicidal thoughts in teenagers.

Let's look at those.

1) *It's fun to be manic* – look at everything you get done. You are happy and self confident, creative and sociable. Nothing can go wrong. However, there is another side – you are also aggressive, embarrassing, have poor judgment, ignore your responsibilities, and hurt others emotionally and physically. Ask if others like being around you when you are manic.

2) *Don't know they need them-* Depression is not something you can snap out of – you have a physical problem even though it's in your brain. Can you tell if you behave or feel differently when you take your meds? Ask your parents if they can tell the difference. If they can tell, then the meds make a difference and you better take them.

If they can't tell, then maybe you aren't on the right meds or aren't taking enough. Also, it can take several weeks for the drugs to take effect. Anyway, it's really hard to tell which meds will work for you specifically and lots of times, the doctors can't get it right on the first try. Also, your body is changing – have you noticed the normal changes happening to you? Well, when that happens, it may change your needs for medication too. It is like shooting at a moving target at the arcade. Except you are blindfolded and can't see the target. So give the doctors a break!

3) *Side effects*
   You might hear about side effects with your medications. There can be all kinds of different symptoms like nausea, jitters, tremors, weight gain, thirst, dry mouth, or the need to go to the bathroom frequently. Usually these will lessen over time. If not, ask your doctor if there is something you can do. For instance, if the medicine makes your stomach feel sick, eat something first. The other side effect may be a decrease in your sexual libido. This may be a good thing because you need to focus on healing yourself, not the complications that come from a teenage sexual relationship.

4) *Denial of the problem* – Do you know what the number one symptom of bipolar depression is – Denial! How is that for a strange disease? It makes you think you don't even have it. The name for the lack of insight that you have a brain disorder is "anosognosis". Well, if someone gave you this book, they think there is a problem. Trust them.

5) *Too depressed to take them* – sometimes when someone is very depressed, everything can be an extreme effort. At my lowest point, I have waited four hours before getting up the energy to go into the bathroom and would not have moved even if you yelled "fire!" If this is your problem, tell your parents so they can bring the meds to you at the right time.

6) *Fear of becoming dependent on them.* That was my biggest fear – I was afraid I would become addicted. Well, a diabetic is not addicted to insulin, but that doesn't mean they don't need to use it. Anti-depressants and drugs for bipolar do not cause you to need them like the nicotine in cigarettes do. However, your illness may require you to use them for a long time. If you are depressed, your feelings could last from 6 months to your entire life. And, if you are bipolar, you need to face the fact that you do have a lifelong illness and medications will become part of that life.

7) *Smart enough to figure it out on your own.* My son was brilliant – he scored at the highest level possible on IQ tests. When he was first suicidal, he called the help line and took meds for a year. He felt better so he stopped. When the suicidal urges returned, he thought he was smart enough to figure it out on his own. Depression is not something you power through or figure out. It is a chemical imbalance. He did the dumbest thing ever the morning he jumped off the bridge to end his pain.

8) *The bottles and TV commercials say that meds might increase the possibility of suicidal thoughts in teenagers.* Anti-depressants treat depressed people. Many of those people have suicidal thoughts. It is hard to know which is the chicken and which is the egg. The medications might have taken someone who was so depressed that they couldn't move and made them more energetic. Once

they have the energy, they are more capable of acting on suicidal thoughts.

There are some frightening statistics that were just released, however. Suicides had *declined* by 22%, coinciding with the *increase* of medications among teenagers. In 2003, they started putting the warnings on the medication which deterred many depressed teenagers from taking antidepressants. Since 2003, there has been the **largest jump in suicides in 15 years** – instead of declining, the rate increased by 8%. (CAREY, 2007) In fact, sadly, suicide is the **third leading cause of death** among Americans who are 15-24. (htt)

Here are the medications I take:

Medicine	When	How much? What it is supposed to do?

There is an important medication guide at the end of this workbook that is the same information provided by the FDA when you receive your medication. **Make sure you tell someone if you experience the feelings it describes!**

One more thing about medications – make sure you only take medication that is prescribed for you. DO NOT take your friend's medications! Each medication has a special dosage and must be measured just for you.

AM I THE ONLY ONE WITH THIS ILLNESS?

Guess what? Look at 10 people in a crowd. Three of those 10 people will have depression during their lifetime.

What color are your eyes?

_____

Have you ever broken a bone?

_____

Have you ever had a cold?_____

Are you embarrassed about any of these? Well, you shouldn't be embarrassed about your mental illness either.

Fill this out:

I am _____. I am _____tall, _____ years old, and have _____ eyes. I also have a silent disability. These all **describe** me, but they do not **define** me. My best features: Inside_____   Physical_____

In history, there were lots of theories about people with mental illness. Originally, society thought that it was caused by an imperfect soul because the person had angered God. Then, they believed that the person was possessed by devils and demons. After that, they accused the person of witchcraft. Later in history, mental illness was thought to be everything from a sign of genius to a lack of self-discipline to self-anger. Now, we know it is biochemical like diabetes.

Now, look at the list of people on the next few pages. Check the ones you have heard of. Try to figure out their greatest accomplishment.

Politicians
John Adams (D)
Franklin Pierce (A)

Rutherford B. Hayes (D)
Menachim Begin (MD)
Winston Churchill (MD)
Oliver Cromwell (MD)
Abraham Lincoln (D)
Theodore Roosevelt(D)
Thomas Eagleton (MD)
George Washington (D)
Empress Elisabeth of Austria (MD,ED)
King Ludwig of Germany (D)
Princess Diana (D,ED)
Richard Nixon (D)
Eleanor Roosevelt (D)
Calvin Coolidge(D)
Lyndon Johnson (D)
George Stephanopoulos (D)
Boris Yeltsin (D, A)
Joseph McCarthy (A)
John Tower (A)
Barbara Bush (D)
Robert McFarlane (D)
Tipper Gore (D)

Creatives
Patty Duke (MD)
Beethoven(MD)
Leonardo de Vinci
Mike Wallace (D)
Ted Turner (MD)
Edgar Allen Poe (MD)
Vincent van Gogh (MD)
Ernest Hemingway (MD/A)
F. Scott Fitzgerald (A)
Hector Berlioz (MD)
Isaac Newton (MD)
Charles Dickens (MD)
Paula Abdul (ED)

Kate Beckinsale (ED)
Joan Rivers (D)
William Styron (D)
Jim Morrison (A)
Rod Steiger (D)
Rona Barrett (D)
Robert Downey Jr. (MD)
Margot Hemingway (MD)
Anne Heche (D)
Tobey Maguire (A)
Mel Gibson (A, MD)
Martin Sheen (A)
Sylvia Plath (D)
Freddie Prinze (D)
Leo Tolstoy (D)
Jack London (A)
Johann Goethe
Danny Kaye (D)
Marilyn Monroe (D)
Lindsey Lohan
Britney Spears (MD)
John Denver (D)
Claude Monet (D)
Robert Schumann (MD)
Virginia Wolff (MD)
Charley Pride (MD)
Art Buchwald (MD)
Rosemary Clooney (MD)
Ned Beatty (MD)
Carrie Fisher (MD)
Robin Williams (MD, A)
Kristy McNichol (MD)
Eugene O'Neill (D)
John Keats (D)
Tennessee Williams (D)
Michelangelo
Vivien Leigh (MD)

Sarah McLachlan(D)
Sheryl Crow(D)
Elton John(D)
Janet Jackson(D)
Jim Carrey(D)
Harrison Ford (D)
Rosie O'Donnell (D)
Hans Christian Andersen (D)
Honore de Balzac
James Barrie
William Faulkner
F. Scott Fitzgerald
Maxim Gorky
Hermann Hesse
Henrik Ibsen
Henry James
Mark Twain (D)
Joseph Conrad
Charles Dickens (D)
Isak Dinesen
Ralph Waldo Emerson
Herman Melville
Mary Shelley (D)
Robert Louis Stevenson
August Strindberg (MD)
Truman Capote (D)
Emile Zola
George Frederic Handel (MD)
Gustav Mahler
Modest Mussorgsky
Sergey Rachmaninoff
Giocchino Rossini
Peter Tchaikovsky (D)
George Gershwin (MD)
Irving Berlin
Noel Coward
Stephen Foster

Cole Porter (D)
Charles Schultz (D)
Toulouse-Lautrec (D,A)
Kurt Cobain (MD)
Robert Burns
George Gordon, Lord Byron (MD)
Samuel Taylor Coleridge
Emily Dickinson (D)
T.S. Eliot
Victor Hugo
Samuel Johnson
John Keats
Edna St. Vincent Millay
Boris Pasternak
Ezra Pound
Alexander Pushkin
Percy Bysshe Shelley
Alfred, Lord Tennyson
Dylan Thomas
Walt Whitman
Paul Gauguin
Edvard Munch
Georgia O'Keeffe(D)
Jackson Pollock (D)
Dick Cavett (MD)
Connie Francis (MD)
Peter Gabriel
Shecky Greene (MD)
Spike Mulligan
Axl Rose (MD)
Jonathon Winters (MD)
Ray Charles (D)
Eric Clapton (D)
Dick Clark (D)
Francis Ford Coppola (MD)
Michael Crichton (D)
Mike Douglas (D)

Mariette Hartley (D)
Anthony Hopkins (D)
Bonnie Raitt (D)
Roseanne Barr (D)
James Taylor(D)
Livingston Taylor(D)
Nick Nolte (A)
Tim Allen (A)
Marie Osmond (D)
Donny Osmond (D)
Danny Bonaduce (MD)
Larry Flynt(MD)
Stuart Goddard (Adam Ant) (MD)
Linda Hamilton (MD)
Margot Kidder (MD)
Tony Orlando (MD)
Ben Stiller (MD)
Gordon Sumner (Sting) (MD)
Jean-Claude Van Damme (MD)
Brian Wilson (MD)
Marvin Lee Aday (Meat Loaf) (D)
Halle Berry (D)
Marlon Brando (D)
Drew Carey (D)
Sarah Ferguson, Duchess of York (D)
Janet Jackson (D)
Billy Joel (D)
Ashley Judd (D)
Jessica Lange (D)
Ozzy Osbourne (D, A)
Kelly Osbourne (A)
Jack Osbourne (A)
Dolly Parton (D)
Neil Simon (D)
Paul Simon (D)
Tracey Gold (ED)
Jamie-Lynn Discala (ED)

Karen Carpenter (ED)
River Phoenix (A)
Edward Furlong (A)
Anthony Michael Hall (MD)
Winona Ryder (D,ED)
Gwyneth Paltrow (D)
Drew Barrymore (D, A)
Alanis Morrisette (D)
Dana Plato (A)
David Strickland (MD)
Mary-Kate Olsen (ED)
Jane Pauley (MD)
Brooke Shields (D)
Anne Rice (D)
Larry King (D)
Oprah Winfrey (D)
Sandra Dee (D)
Howard Stern (D)
Mariah Carey (D)
Norman Rockwell (D)
Ellen DeGeneres (D)
Bobby Darin (D)
Sally Field (D)
Britney Spears (MD)
Mary Tyler Moore (A)
Margaret Cho (D)

Others
Buzz Aldrin (MD)
Erin Brokovich (ED)
Stephen Hawking (D)
John Kenneth Galbraith (D)
Terry Bradshaw (D)
Kitty Dukakis(MD)
Greg Louganis (D)
Daryl Strawberry (MD)
Ilie Nastase (MD)

Meriwether Lewis (of Lewis and Clark) D
Thomas Edison (D)
Florence Nightingale (D)
Charles Darwin (D)
Ralph Nader (D)
George S. Patton (D)
Sigmund Freud (D)
Geoff Gallop (D)
JP Morgan (D)
Isaac Newton (D)
Martin Luther (D)
Socrates (D)

Had you heard of very many of them? You can look them up on the Internet or in an encyclopedia if you need to.

Did you list their greatest accomplishment? I bet you didn't. As a clue, try to identify the speaker of this quote,

"I am now the most miserable man living. If what I feel were equally distributed to the whole human family, there would not be one cheerful face on earth. Whether I shall ever be better, I cannot tell. I awfully forebode I shall not. To remain as I am is impossible. I must die or be better, it appears to me."

Who do you think wrote this?   _____

What was he feeling?   _____

These words were spoken by the 16th president of the US, Abraham Lincoln, who had suicidal depression during much of his life. And you will notice he is on the list on the previous page. In fact, every person on that list has reportedly suffered from some form of mental illness (people in history cannot be diagnosed after the fact, but their behaviors give some evidence). Here are the codes ➢ D - Depressive; MD - Manic Depressive; A - Alcoholic or addict; S-Schizophrenic; ED – Eating disorder.

So, their greatest accomplishment was contributing to the world despite their disability.

You will notice a lot of very creative people on the list. The researchers have done studies. About 30% of people will show some kind of mental illness during their life. However, when they look at **creative** people, 7 out of every 10 of them show some mental illness. (Flaherty, 2004)

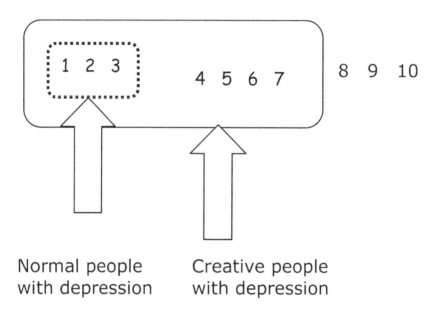

Normal people
with depression

Creative people
with depression

Another study found that poets had a 20% higher suicide rate than others (Jamison, 1994). They turned their torture into something that will impact others positively. Think of the stories of Edgar Allen Poe or the pictures from the mind of van Gogh or the nonstop stand-up comedy from Robin Williams. They have channeled their disability into a gift.

How are you creative?_____

_____

How can you use your illness?_____

_____

_____

WHY ME?

There seems to be **a strong link of mental illnesses in families**. They have done studies on identical twins (who share the same DNA) and 60% of the time, when one has a mental illness, the other one does too. (Finegold) Estimates are that 90% of bipolar people have an affected relative. (Christine T. Finn) That means you don't have to get it, but you should be on the lookout for it if your parents, siblings or grandparents have it. Like some forms of cancer, you may be susceptible to it. Then if something bad happens to you, it may trigger the depression to emerge.

Here are some common triggers that can cause your depression or bipolar depression to emerge – do any apply to you?

Death in the family
Alcoholism in the family
Physical, emotional, or sexual abuse
Lack of money
Lack of parental support system
Academic pressures
Perfectionism
Struggles with peers, bullies
Low self-esteem
Health problems
Pregnancy
Drugs (Illegal or prescribed)
Lack of direction
Major changes like moving homes or schools
Parental divorce or marital conflict
New stepparent
Community violence
School difficulties
Holidays and anniversaries
Loneliness
Job difficulties
Weight

Acne
Late in maturing physically
Caretaker of the family
Legal problems
Traumatic breakup
Trouble with the police
Graduation
Traumatic world events (terrorism, war, hurricanes)
Hormones
Concerns about sex
Sexual identification issues (am I gay?)
Just the accumulation of little stresses

Keep in mind that these causes can trigger the illness of depression with which this workbook will help. However, you will also need to *deal with the trigger itself.* For example, you may need to talk to a therapist as you deal with grief or abuse. If you have questions about your sexuality, there are resources as well. Some books, Web sites, and hotlines are listed at the end of the workbook under *Resources.*

If this discussion hasn't convinced you that this is an illness and not just something in your mind, new studies have shown that bipolar people have a smaller amygdala (a small part of the brain in the front temporal lobe). (Isabelle M Rosso, Vol. 57, No. 1. (1 January 2005)) They can actually see the differences in the brain. Also, scans of depressed brains and regular brains actually **look** different. In autopsies, they have found a lower level of serotonin and an elevated level of cortisol, a stress related hormone. SO, it isn't in your **mind**, it is in your **brain**. It is just like if someone has a **heart** attack, that doesn't mean they can't **love**.

Look at it this way. If you do things that are bad, it could either be because you are bad or because you are sick. Which would you rather be?

BAD   SICK

WHAT DOES DEPRESSION FEEL LIKE?

SYMPTOMS

Let's talk about the symptoms of your illness. I found the main one was *"anhedonia"*. I like that word because it is the opposite of hedonism. It means that one cannot get pleasure from anything that would normally please someone. One little word sums up the main symptom of those of us who are depressed.

If you are **depressed**, these are some of the "official" symptoms listed in the DSM IV.

In psychological talk	In English
Depression	
1. **Depressed mood most of the day nearly every day (May also be irritability in children)**	Feeling totally empty all day every day, dark, hollow, miserable, hopeless, useless; little things annoy you.
2. **Markedly diminished interest or pleasure in almost all activities most of the day nearly every day**	Nothing makes you happy, apathy, everything is boring or dumb
3. **Significant weight loss or gain**	Losing or gaining weight different than usual and without trying
4. **Insomnia/hypersomnia nearly every day**	Sleeping too much or not at all

In psychological talk	In English
5. **Psychomotor agitation or retardation nearly everyday**	Anxious or sluggish
6. **Fatigue or loss of energy nearly everyday**	Really, really tired and drained like someone unplugged your power cord.
7. **Feelings of worthlessness or excessive or inappropriate guilt nearly every day**	Feeling worthless or guilty, helpless and ugly even though you haven't done anything wrong.
8. **Diminished ability to think or concentrate or indecisiveness nearly every day**	Can't focus or decide things, disorganized and can't concentrate
9. **Recurrent thoughts of death, recurrent suicidal ideation without a plan, or a suicide attempt or a specific plan for committing suicide**	Thinking about death or planning it, want to disappear, hope to die

Check the ones you have felt. Did you think you were the only one or that you were weird? Now you know you aren't! And, I know, some of you are saying, "I don't feel like that all of the time – only some of the time – so I don't have it". Well, think about the last few colds you had. Sometimes they were horrible and sometimes they were just annoying. Well, depression can work the same way. If you have mild depression, it is called "Dysthymia". (dis-thigh'-me-ah) You can still get help.

Here is a web questionnaire that will help you assess your symptoms. **Make sure you share this information with your parents or a health professional.**
http://www.dbsalliance.org/site/PageServer?pagename=about_depressionscreener

SUICIDAL THINKING
Do you ever feel like your family would be better off without you?_____
Why?_____
Ask **them** if they would be better off. Write down their responses and read it over next time you feel like that._____

_____
_____
_____
_____

Have you made a plan for suicide?_____
What is it?_____

_____

> THIS IS IMPORTANT!!!
> If you feel like suicide, **GET HELP NOW**!!! If you are too
> embarrassed to ask, fill out the card below and give it to someone
> now!!! **National Adolescent Suicide Hotline 800-621-4000**

HELP CARD
To help you tell someone what you can't say.

PRINT THIS HELP CARD
& Give to your Parent(s) or Other Responsible Adult

> Mom, Dad _____, Help me.
> I am afraid I am going to kill myself.
> If you don't believe me, I could die.
> Please, if you love me,
> Help me.

Ask your parents to help remove temptations related to your plan.
I lived with no knives in my house for 3 years and my gift to myself
when I finally came out of the fog of depression after several years
was a new cutlery set.

Would you like to know what it feels like to lose someone to
suicide? Listen to someone who has gone through it – me. It feels
like your breath is gone – like you want to die. You blame yourself
– if only I had known, if only I had done something different. Lots
of crying and anguish and it just doesn't go away. Of course, there
is the person's body to deal with. Did you know that your body

releases everything when you die? So the people you love the most have to clean up your pee and your poop and your blood. Then they have to throw out the mattress or the carpet so it won't get maggots. Every time they close their eyes, they picture the coroner coming out of the examination room trying not to throw up because the medical examiner had to pull your face off your skull to do the autopsy. Suicide is not glamorous and it doesn't solve anything. My special friend died 17 years ago and my son died on Christmas, 2009 and I miss them each and every day. Every time I do something, I wish I could share it with them or wonder what they would think. The pain NEVER goes away. They will NEVER be better off without you.

Complete the sentence: If I found my_____ had died by suicide, I would feel like_____
_____. Now remember, you don't want your loved ones to feel that way. Still, you brain might tell you to do it.

If you ever feel the urge, **there is help** – THE PAIN WILL GO AWAY WITHOUT HURTING YOURSELF. The next pages list the steps to get help. **DO THOSE STEPS.** Because we want you to stick around.

Remember, 90% of the teens who die by suicide have a treatable mental illness, primarily depression. (Shaffer, 1996) SUICIDE IS A PERMANENT SOLUTION TO A TEMPORARY PROBLEM!!!!!

By the way, sometimes teens cut themselves or hurt themselves rather than try to die by suicide. We know that this self-mutilation is a way to express anger and pain. The physical pain replaces the emotional pain for a little while. This self-abuse is very harmful as well. There is a web site called www.selfinjury.com or a hotline 1-800-DONTCUT that can help you get help.

Let's make a suicide contract now.

I,_____, hereby agree that I will not harm myself in any way, attempt suicide, or die by suicide.

Furthermore, I agree that I will take the following actions if I am ever suicidal:

1) I will remind myself that I can never, under any circumstances, harm myself in any way, attempt suicide, or die by suicide.

2) I will call **911** or **1-800-SUICIDE (800-784-2433)** if I believe that I am in immediate danger of harming myself.

3) I will call any or all of the following numbers if I am not in immediate danger of harming myself but have suicidal thoughts. No one will think I am weak or bad for asking for help.

Signed,_____Date:_____

Friends or family to call for help: Phone:

_____

_____

(Make sure you have told these friends about this contract – they might want to read the book: *Power to Prevent Suicide: A Guide for Teens Helping Teens*")

OR

My Doctor:_____Phone:_____

OR

these suicide hotlines

1-800-SUICIDE (800-784-2433)

1-800-273-TALK

1-800-442-HOPE (4673)

Local teen hotline:_____

OR

911

(A copy of this to cut out is at the end of this workbook)

BIPOLAR DISORDER

Another form of depression is called bipolar disorder. Those who suffer from this illness cycle between the symptoms of depression listed in the previous pages and mania below. In kids and teens, this cycling may happen very quickly (like every 10 minutes).

These are some of the symptoms of the manic side of **bipolar disorder.** If you have not been diagnosed with bipolar disorder, but you feel several of these symptoms, you might want to tell your parents or caregiver so they can evaluate to see if you need more help. Unfortunately, the estimate is that half the people who are bipolar are untreated. (Briefing paper,What percentage of individuals with severe psychiatric disorders are receiving no treatment?, 2007) A lot of times, bipolar disorder is *misdiagnosed* as other conditions such as conduct disorder (CD), oppositional disorder (ODD), attention deficit disorder (ADD), borderline personality disorder, and intermittent explosive disorder. Also, they have determined that 1/3 of teenagers diagnosed with depression may actually be bipolar. (Dec) The problem with this is that the medications that treat depression may throw someone who is bipolar into manic mode.

BIPOLAR SYMPTOMS

In psychological talk	*In English*
Mania	
1. **Inflated self–esteem or grandiosity**	Think you are all that.
2. **Decreased need for sleep**	Can get by with only a little bit of sleep night after night
3. **More talkative than usual**	Chatterbox
4. **Flight of ideas or subjective experience that thoughts are racing**	Your mind is thinking about all kinds of things incessantly.
5. **Distractibility**	Easily distracted – oh, look, there is a chicken.
6. **Increase in goal-directed activity**	Focus on one thing to the exclusion of everything else

In psychological talk	In English
7. Excessive involvement in pleasurable activities that have a high potential for painful consequences (shopping sprees, strong sexuality, foolish business investments)	Doing all the fun stuff, but doing it too much or compulsively.

Here is a web questionnaire that will help you determine if you are bipolar – make sure you share the results with your parents or medical professionals!
http://www.dbsalliance.org/site/PageServer?pagename=about_maniascreener

BIPOLAR BEHAVIORS

The symptoms listed above can cause the following **behaviors**. Check the ones you see in yourself. Ask your parents to see if they think your list is complete. Sometimes we can't see symptoms in ourselves as well as outsiders can. Again, you might want to do this even if you have not been diagnosed as bipolar and let your parents know if you have a lot of these behaviors.

Temper tantrums ☐
Hyperactivity ☐
Skipping school ☐
Inappropriate sexual behavior ☐
Talking fast ☐
Excessively talking ☐
Stealing ☐
Fighting ☐
Excessive risk taking ☐
Lack of remorse (don't feel sorry) ☐
Racing thoughts ☐
Periods of sadness ☐
More withdrawn than normal ☐
Unusually clingy ☐
Irritable ☐
Sleep less than usual ☐

Sleep more than usual ☐
Increased aggression ☐
Arrogant ☐
Unable to focus ☐
Decreased attention span ☐
Unusually happy for no reason ☐
Excessively self-confident ☐
Excessive or loud laughter ☐
Preoccupied with self ☐
Disregard for authority ☐
Grandiose ☐
Cruel ☐
Cutting on Yourself ☐
Destruction of property ☐
Trouble with the law ☐
Frequent lying ☐
Bizarre behavior ☐
Low self-esteem/sense of worthlessness ☐
Cry more easily than usual ☐
Feeling sluggish ☐
Excessive guilt ☐
Change in appetite ☐
Thinking about suicide ☐
Suicide attempt ☐
Night terrors ☐
Paranoid ☐
More anxious than usual ☐
Thinking about sex a lot ☐
Obsessive thoughts ☐
Hearing voices ☐
Excessive risk taking ☐
Constant headaches or stomach aches without cause ☐
Know it all ☐
Need little food ☐
Not feeling like seeing friends ☐
Know-it-all ☐
Invincible ☐

Feel like you have special powers ☐
Shopping sprees ☐

Let's talk about some of the hardest bipolar behaviors to cope with. Unfortunately, while they may lessen, they will still be around once you start taking the medication. This list should help you to be able to recognize them and cope with them easier.

Impulsive thinking – doing things without thinking about the consequences

What is something you have done without thinking it through first? _____

_____

What was the result?_____

_____

List 3 things you have been tempted to do

1._____

2._____

3._____

Write down the possible consequences. _____

_____

Can you deal with these consequences? _____

_____

Difficulty connecting a behavior with a consequence

What is the consequence of not going to school?_____
_____
Not getting your degree?_____
Stealing?_____

What is the consequence of that consequence?_____
_____
Is it worth it?_____
What can you do to try to think things out a little more?
_____

Need for immediate gratification

Name something you wanted recently_____
_____
When did you ask for it?_____
Were you able to wait for it?_____
Make a list of things worth waiting for   _____
_____

Let's make a scale to use in the future – when you want something, check over your scale.

1) *Have to have* (Safety, health, it's the law, school requires it)
2) *Want to have* (weigh your desire vs. the inconvenience to others)
3) *Nice to have* (a luxury)
4) *Lower priority*

Lying

What is a lie you told recently?_____
_____

Does lying really hurt anyone?_____
_____

Here are some things to think about. What if you lie and:
1) Someone else gets blamed
2) Someone else gets hurt
3) You get caught in the lie
4) You can't remember what is not true and what is true.
5) You later tell the truth but no one will believe you?

Here are some tips to tell the truth:
1) Commit to telling the truth and tell others of your commitment.
2) Watch out for exaggeration, white lies, and times where you don't tell the full truth.
3) Consider the consequences if you feel like lying.

Related to telling the truth:
Has someone said that you did one thing and you know you did something else?_____
What if that person is right – could your brain have changed the truth in your head?_____
What if I told you your brain can protect itself by changing reality if it can't deal with the consequences? Ask your parent about an instance where you did something wrong. Listen to them describe it and then say what you think happened. Compare the differences.

Inability to accept blame

When was the last time you did something wrong?_____
_____

Did you blame someone else?_____

Have you ever done something wrong?_____

Write down something you might have done wrong._____

_____

_____

What would it feel like if someone always blamed you?_____

_____

We are telling you about these behaviors so you can realize what you are doing and try to counteract it. Let me also say that your illness provides an <u>explanation</u> when you do bad things, but it is NOT an <u>excuse</u>. You cannot kill someone and then say, sorry, I have a mental illness. **That person is still dead**. It is ultimately your responsibility to ask for help or to accept help when it is offered. It is really hard to accept help sometimes because it is like admitting we are weak or a failure. This is NOT the time to be macho or independent. Ask for help so you don't hurt yourself or others.

Think about this statement –

"Everybody, sooner or later, sits down to a banquet of consequences". What do you think Robert Louis Stevenson meant when he wrote this?

_____

_____

Dealing with Sleepy, Weepy, and Doc or How do I cope?

1) Get honest with yourself

Have you done something you were ashamed of because of the illness?_____

Were you sorry at the time? _____

What did you feel?_____

Whom did you blame?_____

Really, now, whom did you blame? _____

What could you have done differently? _____
_____

Note: If you have hurt someone, it is **NEVER** your victim's fault. It sure is easier to shift the blame to the victim. Yes, they might have annoyed you or not backed off, but NO ONE deserves to be hurt. Sadly, they have found that many of the victims are the people the aggressors love most. Because they know that the victim's love for them is unconditional and will never waiver, they become a *safe* person to abuse.

What do you wish you could tell your victim?_____

Why didn't you?_____

Do you think they need to know?_____

Do you love them?_____

How can you signal this to them?_____

What about asking for forgiveness?_____

Can you forgive yourself?_____

If you decide to make amends to your victim, here are some options:

- Apologize
- Explain your illness (not as an excuse, but as an explanation)
- Make financial amends
- Send an "I'm sorry" card
- Correct the situation if possible
- Be honest about what happened

It is very **difficult** to **rebuild trust**. However, it can be done. Here are some steps:

1) Never break a confidence.
2) Do not lie.
3) Act consistently.
4) Do not go back on a commitment.
5) Have patience. It takes a long time to build trust and only a second to destroy it.

My son had a wonderful observation regarding getting honest with himself:

"Today I woke up feeling disgusted with myself. I deserve it because I brought it on myself. My dad and my teacher and others talk about how they felt bulletproof when they were teens. This is how I have been feeling lately. Respect comes my way, but not how it should. I think respect should come by your person, you know, how a friend respects a friend cause you are there for them. My respect comes to me because I think I scare people. I need to calm down and check myself before I get in a spot I can't handle."

2) PICK-ME-UPS

Keep these options nearby for when you become down or manic. Ideally, you would do these when you first feel the symptoms coming on to prevent them.

☺ Write down a list of songs that make you happy or make you think. See if someone can burn a CD with them for you.

☺ Are there pictures that make you smile? Put them in a photo album that you can keep nearby when you need the support.

☺ What about poems or books or movies? Keep a list here. So what if you've watched the same movie 20 times! I've seen Braveheart 56 times – every time I felt like dying, it picked me up by reminding me about the passion of my lost love who died by suicide.

☺ Take some magazines and make 2 collages of what your life is like now and what you want your life to look like. Notice the colors and the words and the pictures and the placement of all of the components. What does that tell you?_____
_____

☺ Ask your friends to write a paragraph about what they like about you. Save them to look at when you are low.

☺ Write down a list of activities that will use up your extra manic energy, calm you down, or cause you to gain energy. Does something need to be cleaned or is there somewhere you can run? Here are some options:

A long bath
Exercise
Sports
Walking
Volunteering
Traveling
Reading
Writing poetry or in a journal
Meditating
Prayer
Yoga

Being active not only has physical benefits, but also psychological ones. Exercise releases serotonin, which is lacking in depressed individuals. It also releases dopamine which keeps us motivated.

☺ Read this paragraph:
…he referred to the dates on her tombstone from the beginning to the end…What mattered most of all was the ***dash*** between those years. For that dash represents all the time that she spent alive on earth…and now those who love her know what that little line is worth.
How do you want people to describe your "dash"?

_____
_____
_____

☺ If you feel spirituality can help you, then prepare some Bible verses or quotes from books that you can look at. Spirituality tells us that you do not need to fight this battle by yourself – God can minister to you. His spirit is with you always – you just need to seek it. Here are some verses to get you started:

I lift my eyes up to the hills – where does my help come from? My help comes from the Lord, the Maker of heaven and earth. Psalm 121:1-2

For surely I know the plans that I have for you, declares the Lord, plans for good and not for disaster to give you a future and a hope. Jeremiah 29:11

What good will it be for a man if he gains the whole world yet forfeits his soul? Matthew 16:26

This day I call heaven and earth as witnesses against you that I have set before you life and death, blessings and curses. Now **choose life** so that you and your children may live and that you may love the Lord your God, listen to His voice, and hold fast to Him. (Deuteronomy 30:19-20)

If you don't relate to the language used in the Bible, you might want to look at "*The Message*" which is the Bible in contemporary language. Here is an example from 1Peter 5:10:

New International Version: And the God of all grace, who called you to his eternal glory in Christ, after you have suffered a little while, will himself restore you and make you strong, firm and steadfast.
The Message: The suffering won't last forever. It won't be long before this generous God who has great plans for us in Christ—eternal and glorious plans they are!—will have you put together and on your feet for good. He gets the last word; yes, he does.

Another verse from "The Message":
No test or temptation that comes your way is
beyond the course of what others have had to face.
All you need to remember is that God will never
let you down; he'll never let you be pushed past
your limit; he'll always be there to help you come
through it. 1Corinthian 10:13

3) ASK FOR HELP.

It's hard to ask for help. It might mean we are weak. But guess what? Everyone is weak sometimes. So what? Who is the strongest person you know?_____ Ask them to tell you about a time they needed to ask for help. _____
Also, it is important to know that if you wait too long to ask for help, you might go past the point of no return and not be able to ask.

Put together your list of helpers and keep a copy by the phone.

Suicide Hotline_____   _____
Therapist_____
Psychiatrist_____
Friend_____
Friend_____
Church_____
Others_____
_____
_____

Therapists and Psychiatrists
Now, I know a lot of people don't want to talk to a therapist – you 'don't want them in your business' or you might be embarrassed. Let's clear a few things up.

Who are these people they want me to see?

A *therapist* talks and listens – they have been trained to help you understand your illness and your issues.

A *psychiatrist* may do the same thing, but they are also a medical doctor – they can prescribe medications.

How can they know what is going on in my head?
First, you may think you are the only one with your problems, but a good therapist has seen it all before. They might have some unique insight. Also, sometimes it is helpful to have someone outside whatever situation you are in to provide perspective. Sort of like with your friends – it's always easier to see the answers to their problems because you aren't personally involved.

It's embarrassing to talk to a stranger.
You might be embarrassed or afraid or annoyed, but a good therapist is not going to judge you. They just want to help. They may (and should) make you take ownership of your issues, but this isn't judgment, this is the first step toward working out the solution. Also, if you tell them that you do not want your parents to hear about your discussions, they will work with you to set up rules about what is private and what must be shared for your safety. So, feel safe to discuss anything with them.

Why don't they talk much and give me tons of advice?
They may actually do more listening then talking, but, trust me, they are leading you toward understanding with their questions. You know how you don't do something when your parent tells you to do it? Well, if the therapist tells you to do something, you might not. But, if their questions help you to see it on your own, you might.

They might tell someone my most private thoughts. Psychiatrists and therapists have rules about keeping your conversations private. They cannot tell your parents or anyone else anything about your discussion. The only exception to this is if you plan to hurt yourself or others. Do not let this stop you from discussing suicidal thoughts with them – they will have a different perspective on it than you do in your depressed mind.

<u>Another possible source of help is God</u>.
A bipolar teen was out of control with drugs and violence, having dropped out of school and repeatedly being arrested. One day, he decided that he would have faith in God and he turned his life totally around. He wrote this prayer to share with others.

<u>The Prayer</u>
This right here is a prayer if you start to fear that the answer isn't clear.

Dear Lord, I know you're awesome.
Please help me with my problems.
I feel like I hit rock bottom.
Tell me why it seems things are causing me
A catastrophe -
Why is the devil chasing after me?
These disastrous things
seem to be the last of me
so give me some protection.
put me in the right direction
to salvation.
Please give me a right way to handle the situation
Keep my mind waves from playing these treacherous games
I seem to want to play
In these wicked ways
I'll obey
What you have to say
Please give me an answer
I feel like I am at the end of my rope
Soak my heart with hope
Help me find a way to cope
Poke a hole through the sheet that is covering me
And I know everything happens for a reason.
But this is seeming like I'm dreaming

Because it seems undeserving
But I know I'm just learning
And it will be worth it
So now I wonder why I worry
Thanks for not letting it get the best of me
Thanks for every one of your blessings
Lord, I need to confess
That my faith almost went down with the rest of me
Thanks for showing me some better things
That you're helping me and protecting me.

Thank you, Lord. Amen.

4) IMPROVING RELATIONSHIPS WITH YOUR FAMILY

Siblings
Everyone gets annoyed by his or her siblings.

Sibling	Annoying things	Nice things	What they must think about me
1.			
2.			
3.			

Here is a prayer written by the younger sister of a bipolar teenager. Do you think your siblings might be feeling the same? Keep in mind that your sisters and brothers will be the last ones standing by your side later on when all your friends are gone. Their love is unconditional, but don't abuse it!

Lord, I don't understand why he acts like this. What did I do? Am I really that bad of a sister? Please keep him safe, and me, too. I'm scared now, I don't want him to have another episode and hurt me, or my mom. This is scary. If only I understood. Why isn't he like "normal" kids? Why does he target me? Why do I have to act differently around him? I can't tease him like I do my other brothers. Doesn't he understand that I am just a kid. I don't know how to not be annoying. I can't even talk around him sometimes because I am afraid that what I say might produce a spark. I hate this feeling, like I have to walk on my tip-toes because anything that I do or say could instigate an explosion. Why did you make him like this, and why did you make me like this, to the point where everything about me annoys him. Is it me? Did I make him like this? I must have, because he always seems to come after me. What was it, then? What horrible crimes have I committed that this would be my punishment? I still love him, Lord. The most important thing I want him to know is that. I still love him, and I hope that he still loves his dear sister, too. Make him better, Jesus. Amen.

List 3 things you can do to improve your relationships with your siblings.

_____

_____

_____

A book that might help your siblings to undestand is "The Sibling Slam Book: What it's Really Like to Have a Brother or Sister with Special Needs" by Don Meyer.

Parents
Everyone gets annoyed by his or her parents, especially teenagers. Let's look at both sides of the story.

Parent Or step parent	Annoying things	Nice things	What they must think about me
1._____			
_____			
2._____			
_____			
3._____			
_____			

Here are some nice things you might not have included:
Unconditional love no matter what you do, protection, discipline, appreciate your strengths, trusting, accepting, understanding, have fun together, communicate with you, encouragement, listening, educate you, go to therapy with you. Have they stuck up for you when the rest of the world didn't? What about at school or with the law or the hospitals or insurance companies or doctors?

Here are some things you might be afraid that your parents think about you. Talk about it with them and see if you are making false assumptions.

> - I contributed to others' depressions, stresses, divorces or failures.
> - They are embarrassed about me, angry at me, afraid of me.
> - They don't want me around, don't trust me, don't understand me.

David Spangler writes, "Parents are the portal through which a human soul becomes part of the world." (Spangler, 1998) You wouldn't be here if not for them! For that alone, they deserve your respect. And, because you are their creation, and, indeed, their contribution to the world, they have unconditional love for you.

I found this amazing song that expressed exactly what I felt about my children – ALL my children including the ones with mental illness.

Find Your Wings
sung by Mark Harris

It's only for a moment you are mine to hold
The plans that heaven has for you
Will all too soon unfold
So many different prayers I'll pray
For all that you might do
But most of all I want to know
You're walking in the truth
And If I never told you
I want you to know
That as I watch you grow -

Drawing by Diana Gomez, 14

Chorus:
I pray that God would fill your heart with dreams
And that faith gives you the courage
To dare to do great things
I'm here for you whatever this life brings
So let my love give you roots
And help you find your wings.

May passion be the wind
That leads you through your days
And may conviction keep you strong
Guide you on your way
May there be many moments
That make your life so sweet
Oh, but more than memories

It's not living if you don't reach for the sky
I'll have tears as you take off
But I'll cheer as you fly.

Is that song perfect or what?

List 3 things you can do to improve your relationships with your parents.

_____

_____

_____

A couple of other activities you might want to add – apologize, discuss feelings with them, monitor your moods, develop a signal system relating to your moods, encouragement, and education about your illness.

Here is a wonderful apology from a bipolar teen –

I Apologize
Dear Mama,
Sorry for the problems I'm causin'
If I harmed ya I apologize
Dry your eyes – I didn't mean to make you cry
I just hope you realize
That I do try
It's been a million times/ I messed up
But you stayed by my side
Don't know why
But I do know that I'm thankful and shameful
That I love you so much I've learned to hate you
You've been there since I was in the cradle
Sorry I've been hateful and unfaithful
I guess time will tell
If we make it or fail
I pray that you won't bail
Cause I need you like brain cells

Are needed or else the brain fails
Two different worlds we're livin' in
One of the past based on facts
And the other one of a new generation/ever-changing
Never seen a perfect family
So we need to adapt to things
Sorry, but that's how things have to be.

There is an Internet support group for family members of people with bipolar depression that you might want to share with your family.
www.bpso.org

5) PEER PRESSURE

If your friends tell you to do something, it is really hard to do something different.

What is something they told you to do that you weren't sure about? What did you do? _____
_____
_____

What could you have done better?
_____
_____
_____

Can you think of someone who did something because of peer pressure that they later regretted or that got them into big trouble?
_____
_____
_____

Now can you tell your friends not to put you in a bad situation?

_____

_____

_____

Ask your parents to make a pact – if you call them and ask to be picked up at any time of the day or night , they will do it if you tell them you are trying to avoid peer pressure to do something bad.

It is important to learn to think for yourself. You might do something in a group, but you will be by yourself when it comes time for your punishment.

6) SUBSTANCE TEMPTATIONS

Substance abuse is not good for any child or teen (or adult for that matter). But, you have no choice – YOU CANNOT take alcohol or illegal drugs if you have a mental illness. It may be hard for you to resist – if you are depressed, you might think it will make you feel better. However, alcohol and these drugs are **depressants** – they will actually bring you down. The researchers have found that 20% of depression is actually caused by substance abuse, not the other way around. And if you are bipolar, you may be tempted to calm the mania in your brain with these substances, but they react very badly with the medications you are on and they can literally combine to kill you. Remember the blood tests they are doing to monitor your liver? Well, what organ do you think alcohol affects?

	Good thing about it	Bad thing about it
Alcohol		
Weed		
Cigarettes		
Xanax		

	Good thing about it	Bad thing about it
Ecstasy		
Other drugs		

There are other reasons why you might be tempted by substances:
Curiosity
A quick fix to your problems
Peer pressure
Loneliness
Danger factor

Do you see any of these factors in your life? Write down other solutions besides drugs and alcohol._____
_____
_____

Alcohol

Of course, drinking and driving is not something you should do at any time, but remember, when you drink and take your medication, it enhances the effect of the alcohol. So you may think you aren't drunk, but you will not have a normal reaction to alcohol and it might take just a very few drops. The same goes for Dayquil and other over-the-counter medications that contain alcohol.

Weed

Lots of people will tell you that weed does not have any bad impact on you. That is **absolutely** wrong!! First of all, the weed you smoke might be laced with something stronger, especially if it's a blunt. But even if it is pure, it's not good for you. STOP! I know you are dismissing what I am about to say just like I did when I was in your position. You might not think it is impacting you until you quit it and look back at others who are still on it and you will see how silly they are acting. Just like your parents can see the impact on you.

Here are some of the effects of weed on your body:

- Your brain – specifically the nerve cells that impact your memory.
Go to this web site to see the exact impact on your brain:
http://www.freevibe.com/Drug_Facts/the_brain.asp And, as the web site says, "You can't get a brain transplant!"

- Your self control – timing and coordination and judgment

- Your lungs – there are 400 chemicals in marijuana and it contains 4X the amount of cancer-causing tar as cigarettes!

- Your immune system – it is harder to fight off infections

- Your mental health – it worsens depression.

A lot of teens might use the argument that since it is natural, it won't hurt you. Well, carbon monoxide and tobacco and cobras are natural too.

It is also addictive to some people, and those with mental illness may be the ones most susceptible to the addiction. A majority of bipolar teens have substance abuse issues. (Child and Adolescent Bipolar Foundation) So don't even start!

Write down the numbers for some local substance abuse programs for teens like Teen AA (Alcoholics Anonymous) and NA (Narcotics Anonymous).
Name Number   Meeting place   Days and times
_____
_____

Here are some contacts:
National Clearinghouse for Drug and Alcohol Information 800-729-6686

http://ncadi.samhsa.gov/
Partnership for a Drugfree America http://www.drugfree.org/
Girl Scouts of America – "In the Zone" drug prevention workbook   800-221-6707
National Institute on Drug Abuse http://www.drugabuse.gov/students.html
Info on Drugs and teens: www.freevibe.com
Quiz to see if you are addicted http://www.freevibe.com/stepup/friendquiz2.asp

Here are some pearls of wisdom from a teen with bipolar who has been intimately acquainted with illegal drugs.

Let me tell you something kid Imma let you in on it / this "disease" and those drugs are a fake promise / Your friends now/ who are around / are they by you when you're feeling down / not just in your presence but on your side / are they down to ride or are they livin' that lie too? / and this "disease", is it just an excuse to run to? / That's what I wanna let you know / that's a weakness to let you not feel capable / get strong in your mind / even if it means leavin' your friends behind / you get what I'm sayin' you are your own witness / get some strength to let you feel like you can wait / I'll say these drugs are an easy way to escape / but what better way to relieve the pressure / than to gain a route through the dilemma / I got to let you know that we all run / but if your head's in the wrong position you're already done / cooked / and finished / take a look at yourself and see if you're your own witness / baby boy you're still growin' / a mind's a terrible thing to waste now you know and get through it you'll be stronger / a bigger boat coastin' through the ocean / lasting longer //

Find yourself and you will know what to do.

Tobacco
Smoking may not impact your illness, but it sure is a slow form of suicide. Go to your car, turn it on, and suck on the tailpipe. Why not? It's the same as smoking. You are having enough

problems with the chemicals in your body – try to keep it as clean as possible.

A friend of mine never thought she would get sick from smoking – in fact, she had never been in a hospital a day in her life. *"It won't happen to me."* She had her last cigarette the day she was diagnosed with lung cancer and given 6 months to live. Her body slowly shut down so she couldn't move or talk. But you could see the fear in her eyes and the tears on her cheeks when I came to say goodbye and apologize because we had not had enough time to travel to the Amazon together as we had dreamed of. She was trapped in her body. Six months and one day after her diagnosis, she was dead. We went to the Amazon, but it was to spread her ashes.

Here are some sources of help for tobacco addiction:
Office on Smoking and Health (CDC) 770-488-5705 www.cdc.gov/tobacco
American Cancer Society 800-ACS-2345   www.cancer.org
American Lung Association 800-586-4872 www.lungusa.org
Nicotine Anonymous 415-750-0328 www.nicotine-anonymous.org
www.thetruth.com

If you are religious, remember these Bible verses:

...don't you know that your body is a temple of the Holy Spirit, who lives in you and was given to you by God? You do not belong to yourself. 1Corinthians 9:25

Who has woe? Who has sorrow? Who has contentions? Who has complaining?
Who has wounds without cause?
Who has redness of eye?
Those who linger over wine
Those who go to taste mixed wine.
Do not look on the wine when it is red,

When it sparkles in the cup,
When it goes down smoothly;
At the last it bites like a serpent,
And stings like a viper.
Your eyes will see strange things,
And your mind will utter perverse things. And you will be like
one who lies down in the middle of the sea,
Or like one who lies down on the top of a mast.
They struck me, but I did not become ill
They beat me, but I did not know it.
When shall I awake?
I will seek another drink.
(Proverbs 23:29-35)

Resolutions about substances
I will not use_____. If I am tempted, I will
call_____.
I will not use_____. If I am tempted, I will
call_____.

7) SELF- EXAMINATION

Everyone wants to be good. But really, what is good? Let's look at
the quality of honesty. You walk into a room and you find a wallet
with $10 and an ID. Do you return the money? What about if it
was $100? What about $1 million? What if you knew you could
get away with it? A truly honest person would return it EVEN if
they could get away with it.

Were you tempted to take the money? What if I told you the
money was for an operation for your best friend's mother? You
never know so do the right thing.

Now, let's look at yourself and your future. What are your hopes
and your dreams? What are your gifts and how can you contribute
to the world in the future_____

Self-examination is also really important when you do something that you later regret. An observation by my son:

"...It's a shame what I did last night. I got high for me, being selfish. I say this because I tell L..... to stay off drugs, I made a promise to E... and to myself that my support would be through me not smoking. It's time for me to be a good influence instead of a therapeutic good deed mediator trying to tell people what's good and bad. I'm not God. Actions speak. An influence is better. The truth is the best. Father, please take the devil out of my words. Please let me use my gift to create, not destroy..."

8) NUTRITION AND ROUTINES

There is some information available that suggests there are some things you can do to improve your health by improving some habits.

1) Food
- Avoid caffeine (this includes cola, coffee, tea, and, sadly, chocolate)
- Avoid sodas
- Avoid processed sugar
- Avoid saturated fat (there go your potato chips)
- Add salads to your diet – there are a lot of fun things you can put on them to make them interesting
- Increase complex carbohydrates like whole grains, pasta, potatoes, and vegetables
- Absolutely avoid alcohol and illegal drugs
- Increase the amount of Omega-3 fatty acids in your diet (you can get this from fish or from capsules you will find in the vitamin section of the store)
- Watch how much you eat. That bag of Oreos sure is tempting, but eating the whole thing won't fix what ails

you. They have found that depression is a major cause of teen obesity – but also that teen obesity is a major cause of depression. In either case, watch the quality and quantity of what you eat.

WARNING:

If you think you are experiencing an eating disorder, ask for help. We know that 50% of those with anorexia are depressed. (Raymond Lemberg, 1999) This book can help you with the depression, but separately, you also have to deal with your eating disorder. It can kill you! In fact 6-10% of those with an eating disorder DIE. These disorders can damage the heart, the esophagus and the gastric system. Here are some questions you need to ask yourself: *Are you terrified about being overweight? Have you gone on eating binges where you felt you might not be able to stop? Do you feel extremely guilty after eating? Do you vomit or have the impulse to vomit after meals? Do you feel that food controls your life? Do you exercise excessively or abuse diet pills or diuretics? Do you gain control of your life by controlling your body?* If any of these apply to you, there are resources in the back of this workbook to guide you.

---

2. Medication
- Avoid nitrous oxide (laughing gas)
- Avoid St.John's wort, Ginkgo Biloba
- Avoid Sudafed
- Depending on your medication, avoid Aleve, Advil, and aspirin
- TAKE YOUR MEDS EVERYDAY!
3. Sleep
- It is very important to get plenty of sleep. Try to go to bed at the same time every night and make sure you get at least 8 hours of sleep.
- I will go to bed at _____ and wake up at _____ on weekdays and _____ on weekends.
- Make yourself get up each morning.
4. Exercise

- Improves your moods, calms you, increases energy and sense of well-being, improves your digestion and eliminates tension. This isn't just a general observation. Studies have demonstrated that exercise breaks down hormones and chemicals that build up from stress as well as releases endorphins that combat depression. Exercise has the added benefits of tiring you out so your sleep is improved and providing something to distract you from your depressed musings. If you find it hard to exercise, try Wii Fit or Wii Sports.

5. Sunshine and light can improve moods
6. Break up tasks into bite size pieces – try to make forward motion each day.

9) REDUCE STRESS /RELAX

Make a list of the stressors in your life. Don't be afraid to put something down if it bothers you – no matter how small. Those might be the easy ones to eliminate. After you have made the list, go over it with your parents or your therapist and see if there are any accommodations that can be made to ease the stress.

Stress relievers
Learn relaxation techniques like yoga
Use music, sound, lighting, scents, and massage
Practice breathing exercises and listen to relaxation tapes. Try the 4-7-8 breathing method. Breathe out for 4 counts, hold it for 7, and then exhale for 8 counts, making a whooshing sound.
Find outlets for stress like exercise, basketball, painting, aerobics, swimming, biking, dancing, singing, watching movies.
Make changes in your life gradually – no crash diets, intense workout programs. True change occurs when you take small steps over a longer period of time since you can maintain the transformation.
Don't watch the local news since it tends to be negative more often than not.

Accept that life can be awkward sometimes – everything does not have to be perfect and on time.

Be patient – give things a chance.

Experience good things now – do not just set goals that are forever in the future. Enjoy life daily.

Stay away from negative people.

Lose yourself in a book.

Enjoy a hobby.

Plant a garden or walk through one.

Take a bubble bath with your favorite body wash.

Blow bubbles.

Play with children.

Make lists and prioritize tasks.

Don't worry until you are sure you have something to worry about.

Visualize a relaxing scene or a good result to your problem.

Listen to others.

Do something different to shake up your routine.

Eat slowly and savor the food.

Forgive others.

Share your feelings.

Do not assume everyone else is judging you. And even if they are, that's their problem, not yours.

See the humor in life. Laugh. Laugh at yourself.

Hug someone for no reason.

Look at the stars.

Open the closed doors of your life. The doors are likely not locked - you may just be assuming they are. Get rid of artificial barriers.

Don't stress over upcoming events. That just means you relive it over and over when it may not even end up being negative.

Think about what good you have done – surely there is something.

Make a scrapbook of things that made you proud of yourself.

Cry.

Write in a diary.

Punch a pillow.

Count your blessings.

Lower your expectations for yourself. Are you being a perfectionist? Does it really matter in the long run if everything is just so?

Some of these hints and others can be found in these books:
"Fighting Invisible Tigers: A Stress Management Guide for Teenagers" by Earl Hipp
"Are you making yourself crazy? – 100 Ways to rid your life of Needless Stress" by G. Gaynor McTigue.
"Too stressed to Think?" By Annie Fox and Ruth Kirschner

Stressor	Potential Fix
_____	_____
_____	_____
_____	_____
_____	_____
_____	_____
_____	_____
_____	_____

10) FORGIVE YOURSELF AND OTHERS.

If someone has done something to hurt you, it is important to forgive them. The more you hold in resentment, YOU are the one who is harmed since it slowly eats away at you. Think about the last time you got angry at a stupid driver. You probably stewed about it for awhile after and got stressed and upset. Meanwhile, the other driver is proceeding along with nothing bothering him. Who is the one who is harmed?

Likewise, if you have done some things that you consider unforgiveable, it is important to release that. The first step is to make a list of those people that you feel you have harmed. After that, it might be helpful to role play with someone the process of apologizing. If you feel strong enough, you can then make amends and apologize to the injured party. If you do not feel strong enough emotionally to actually apologize, you could write a letter. Even if you never deliver it, it frequently makes you feel better just getting it out of you. The final suggestion to help you toward forgiveness is to talk with a religious counselor. Forgiveness is a major theme in many religions and they can share that perspective with you.

11) LOOK AT YOUR LIFE THROUGH A DIFFERENT SET OF GLASSES.

Thomas Edison's lab was destroyed in 1914 and he lost all his work. Instead of going into despair, he said "All our mistakes have been burnt up. Thank goodness we can start anew." Three weeks later he produced his first phonograph. Lee Iacocca, a former head of Chrysler Corporation, said, "We are continually presented great *opportunities* brilliantly disguised as *insoluble problems.*" And, Claire Booth Luce observed, "There are no hopeless situations, there are only those who have grown hopeless about them."

What are some of your *"opportunities"*?_____
_____
_____
_____

How can you grow from them?

_____
_____
_____
_____

12) WORK ON YOUR SELF-ESTEEM.

Do you feel like any of these apply to you?

I am ugly.
I am worse than others.
I will fail at things I try.
I'm afraid to deal with others.
Others will criticize me.

I am always finding fault with myself.
I am filled with guilt and shame.
I don't take care of myself.
I am inferior to others.
I can't do anything right.
I am afraid of what others think about me.

If so, you may suffer from low self-esteem. You need to remember that you are unique and you are special. EVERY SINGLE PERSON IS so why would it be different for you?

Here are some actions you can do to work on your self-esteem.
1) Find a support system – hang out with others that will praise you and have unconditional caring for you.
2) Be a good friend. That will come back to you.
3) Accept praise from others. Really accept it – why would they lie?
4) Learn some new skills to improve yourself – music or arts and crafts or whatever you love to do.
5) Go to therapy and address the issue there.
6) Dress nicely – looking good can help you feel good.
7) Set goals for the future and act on them.
8) Get a pet – dogs love you no matter what.
9) Try new things.
10) Avoid people who bring you down and criticize you.
11) At the same time, don't assume that someone is going to criticize you.
12) Focus on your past successes and the positive.
13) Give yourself credit – do not assume that you did well because you were lucky or someone else caused it.
14) Find a role model and learn some lessons from them. If you can act like someone you admire, then you should feel better about yourself.
15) Focus on strengths that you have and build them into your life.

16) Try new things and continue with the ones that you like. If it doesn't work out, move onto the next thing and be grateful for the lessons you learned.

17) Try out different groups of people – maybe you will fit in with a certain type that will think like you. (Make sure the group is a "healthy" group for you, however. For example, if you drink too much alcohol, make sure they don't.)

18) Realize you don't have to be perfect. Whose judgment are you afraid of when it gets right down to it? Perhaps your own?

19) Nothing is black and white – find the good in the shades of gray.

20) If something goes wrong, do not think that it proves you are worthless. Say "I made a mistake", not "I am a loser". Also, maybe someone else also had something to do with the failure.

21) Create affirmations for yourself. Read them out loud.

AFFIRMATIONS

Make sure they are in the present tense
Make sure they are in the first person
Make sure they are positive and short.

Some examples:
I am healthy.
I am loved.
I am in charge of my life.
I am valuable.
I am strong.
I accept myself as I am.

Now write some out for yourself:

_____

_____

Post them on your mirror and read them every morning and every night.

13) USE A FILTER ON YOUR WORDS

Often, words will just come out of your mouth without thinking about them. Have you ever said something that you would like to take back?

What did you say and to whom?

_____
_____
_____

Did you mean them?_____
What about at that time?_____
What were the consequences of those words?

_____
_____

If you could have taken them back, would you? _____

A good trick is to pretend that your words need to go through a filter or a sieve.

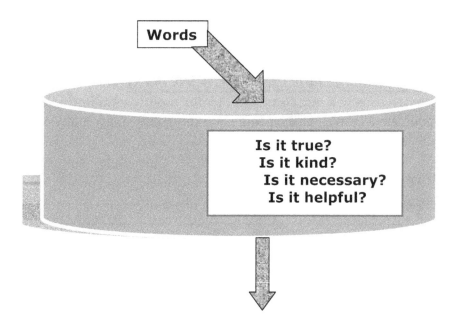

Look back at some of your statements now and see how they would come out through that filter.

Statement   **Filtered Statement**

For example: I hate you ➤ What you said made me angry. Let's try to figure out why.

_____

_____

_____

_____

_____

_____

14) VOLUNTEER

Many of these goals can be accomplished by volunteering. There are many potential organizations, but you can help others with 1) your time, 2) your knowledge, and 3) your caring.

- Check out these Web sites to find volunteer opportunities
  - http://www.volunteermatch.org/

- http://www.networkforgood.org/
- http://www.actsofkindness.org/

- Books about volunteering and making a difference
  - The Teen Guide to Global Action by Barbara A. Lewis
  - The Kids' Guide to Social Action by Barbara A. Lewis
  - The Kid's Guide to Service Projects by Barbara A. Lewis
  - A Kids' Guide to Helping Others Read and Succeed by Cathryn Berger Kaye
  - A Kids' Guide to Hunger and Homelessness by Cathryn Berger Kaye
  - Kids with Courage by Barbara A. Lewis
  - The Doggy Dung Disaster and other True Stories by Garth Sundem

15) LOOK AT THE NEGATIVE IMPACT OF YOUR BEHAVIOR.

What could happen if you continue on your current course? There are many programs available to help you see the future without living it.

- Coroners have programs
- Boot camp "Motivation Day"
- Holocaust Museums
- Victim programs like Justice for All
- Survivors of Suicide http://www.crisishotline.org/how_survivors.html
- Federal Prisons –
  Jail Ministry
  Huntsville death row Texas Prison Museum, 1113 12th St., call (936) 295-2155
- Homeless – shadow a homeless person for a day
- Runaway homes
- Drug/alcohol/tobacco clinics

How do I let others know how I'm feeling?

Part of asking for help is letting people know how you feel. This section will make it easier to do that.

<u>Daily evaluation</u>

Let's set up a code to let everyone know what kind of day you are having. Please know that your mood may change during the day, during different times of the month, and seasonally, with winter being especially bad.

Do you see any patterns to your depression?_____

Depressed – assign a color code to each feeling. Cut out some construction paper and find a place to put the right color so others know how you are feeling. You can also draw a picture on it to illustrate what it feels like.

<u>Feeling</u>   <u>Color Code</u>

Feeling good   _____

Not feeling much of anything   _____

Feeling anxious   _____

Feeling like crying   _____

Feeling like dying   _____

Feeling like raging   _____

There is also a product on www.moodtree.com that will help you chart what you are feeling with colorform apples. (850-386-3455)

Another option is a Mood Swings Flipchart found at www.freespirit.com.

What do you want from others when you are having these feelings? Check the following that apply to you and add any others you might have.

Support through:
__ Reassurance
__ Hugs
__ Affirmations that I am good
__ Listening
__ Forgiveness for your manic acts
__ Prayers

Someone to:
__ Leave me alone to work it out
__ Do things with
__ Keep me safe
__ Encourage me to do things
__ Help with my grooming
__ Be near, but not hovering
__ Do things _____ for me
__ Tell me to slow down
__ Keep me away from drugs and alcohol
__ Read to me

DO NOT:
__ Follow me when I am upset
__ Blame me
__ Desert me
__ Avoid me
__ Tell me to get myself together
__ Pressure me to go out
__ Tell me to cheer up
__ Tell me about how good my life is
__ Tell me about others who have it worse.

For bipolar patients:
Since rage can be dangerous to others, let's put together a specific rage indicator. Make a copy of the chart on the bottom of the page and put it with your mood colors.

Examine your rages and fill out the following hints. SHARE them with the people who surround you.

Mood shift warning signs:_____
When it is shifting, you better:_____
As my mood darkens, I feel like:_____
_____
_____

Trigger list (be specific about what triggers your rage!):
_____   _____
_____   _____
_____   _____

Remember, this does not transfer the blame to the victim!!! You still must isolate yourself and get help if you feel the rage coming on.

Here are some tips for overcoming your rage. How can you use them?

1) Write your feelings down or write a letter to the person. Do not give it to them for at least 2 days and see if it is still appropriate.
2) Don't take the source of your anger personally. Maybe the person was having a bad day or maybe you misunderstood.
3) Go to a safe place to calm down. Make sure you have agreed ahead of time with school or family on a place and that you shouldn't be followed. However, YOU must promise that you will not hurt yourself in this place.
4) Figure out what getting mad will do – what are the benefits – how will it help? And, how might it hurt you or others? What are some possible things you could do instead?
5) Look at the cause of your anger in the scheme of the world. How important is it relative to sad things in the news? If the headlines talked about the subject of your anger, would it be on the front page or buried in the middle?

Feedback scale

Overall

Mild			Mood darkening			Intense	
1	2	3	4	5	6	7	8

Other Dimensions:

Giddy			Happy		Sad		Empty
1	2	3	4	5	6	7	8

Angry			Frustrated			Peaceful	
1	2	3	4	5	6	7	8

Tired						Energized	
1	2	3	4	5	6	7	8

Confused						Thinking Straight	
1	2	3	4	5	6	7	8

What do I do now?

Whether or not you are Christian, read the following. The Bible was written long ago in many languages. The original word in the Bible for "workmanship" was derived from the word, "*poiema* " which is the basis for the word "poem". *For we are God's workmanship, created in Christ Jesus to do good works, which God prepared in advance for us to do. Ephesians 2:10*

Think about the concept of living your life like it is a **poem** – a masterpiece where all the lines blend together to create a beautiful work of art. To do that, we need to set some goals. If you don't know which way you are headed, how are you going to know when you get there? Your goals should be in several areas. When you set those goals, make them specific and put a timetable with them so you can measure your progress. Dream about your perfect life and then try to work toward it in steps that are manageable.
Educational_____

_____

_____

Family_____

_____

Friends_____

_____

Professional_____

_____

Financial_____

_____

Health_____

_____

Travel_____

_____

Physical_____

_____

GOOD GRIEF!

It is scary to find out you have a serious illness. Martin Luther, who suffered chronic depression, once wrote, "I more fear what is within me than what comes from without." That is pretty impressive since he took on the powerful Catholic Church when he hammered his *95 Theses* to the church door in 1546, sparking the Protestant reformation.

So, the normal reaction to finding out you have an illness is *grief*. Life may never be the same. The grieving process can be painful, but it is normal and it actually helps you heal. I do mean "process" because there are several steps, but no timetable to go through them. Grief is uniquely personal.

By the way, this discussion of grief might also help you if grief about a tragic event was one of the triggers that started your depression in the first place.

Stages of grief
1) Denial
   - This can't be happening – a numbness
   - Shock, panic
2) Anger
   - It is easy to blame others or God at this point
   - Crying, screaming
   - Frustration
3) Sadness/depression
   - Fear of change, unknown

- Sense of mortality
- Loss of control
- Loss of what might have been
- Feeling alone

4) Guilt
- Blaming yourself

5) Acceptance

- This is when the pain will lessen
- It is ok to be happy again
- Adjustment to living in the new reality

It is important that others:
1) don't minimize your grieving process
2) understand that grief is a normal response to loss.
3) Don't use clichés such as
   a) Be strong
   b) It is God's will or for the best
   c) Worse things can happen
   d) Time will cure you
4) Don't smother you. However, remember that your parents may be grieving as well. Give them a break.
5) Give you a chance to talk about your grief if you choose. They should just be willing to listen. They do not need to "fix" anything (which will be their first instinct).

It is important that you:
1) Ask for help.
2) Share your feelings - it can be cathartic (make you feel better) and give you insight. If you don't feel comfortable talking to others, write in a journal.
3) Forgive yourself and others – the more you hold in the resentment, YOU are the one who is harmed since it slowly eats away at you.
4) Imagine yourself healing.
5) Exercise, eat well, and take care of yourself.

6) Remember to stay open to the pain – it is not bad. Instead, it is part of life's experience to teach you. A wound that bleeds is cleansing itself to prepare to heal.

7) Transform the painful loss into a gift from which you can learn and grow. You have been pushed off a cliff – you can either fall or soar.

8) Recognize if your grief turns from sadness to depression. Sadness is an emotion – depression is a void. Ask for help if you feel this happening.

9) Understand that nonacceptance does not change the facts. You must accept the reality of the loss.

10) Undergo an attitude adjustment to accept the unacceptable and surmount the unsurmountable.

11) Don't feel guilty if you don't cry or cry too much.

12) Don't play the "*if only*" game. You are not responsible and you could not have changed anything.

13) See if you can help someone else. That may help you get your mind off your own pain.

14) Find a support group. Others who have been through the same experience might be able to help you.

15) Remember you are not alone!

16) Live your life as a tribute to the one who died.

You don't get to choose how you are going to die. Or when. You can only decide how you are going to live. Now.
-Joan Baez (quoted in *When a Friend Dies*)

Here are some books that might help you in your grieving process.

A Teen's Simple Guide to Grief	Alexis Cunningham
After You Lose Someone You Love	Amy, Allie, and David Dennison
Healing Your Grieving Heart for Teens: 100 Practical Ideas	Alan D. Wolfelt, PH. D

Healing Your Grieving Heart Journal for Teens	Alan D. Wolfelt, PH. D
I will Remember You: What to Do When Someone You Love Dies	Laura Dower
When a Friend Dies: A book for Teens about Grieving and Healing	Marilyn Gootman
When Will I Stop Hurting? Teens Loss and Grief	Edward Myers

Is there life after the craziness?

Here are some comments from my bipolar son who has been through drug addiction, police interaction, rehab, mental hospitals, and on and on.

"I've been through it too and I'll tell you it doesn't get easy. But if you open your vision, get stronger, and expand your mind, then you expand your options. It gets rough, but nobody ever said it'll be easy. Start disciplining yourself little by little and before you know, it builds up. It's like you will train yourself to be your own warrior, you know. You'll be alright. Keep your head up."

"If you know it's been done, then what's stopping you?"

Why I Would Not Change Anything About My Life
I wouldn't change anything about my life based on the simple fact that I like the person I have come to be. If I changed any moment of my life (ex: the trouble, failing school, etc.) I would not be where I am, would not think with the experience I have, and I would not be as comfortable as I am about being crazy. I'm crazy and that's what I love about myself. There is nobody who can tell us what is in our future, but one thing is certain: you can do what you do and know that anything that comes is based on your responsibility. This is what makes me comfortable.

Resources

Here are some resources if you want to get more information on mental illness and suicide prevention. This is just a list; we can't assume any responsibility for the information or accuracy of contents provided.

Movies
Manic
Girl, Interrupted
Sylvia
The Hours
Lust for Life
Boys Don't Cry
Sybil
Prozac Nation
Freedom Writers

Books

For teens

Boy Who Drank Too Much	Alcohol	Shep Greene
Charming Billy	Alcohol	Alice McDermott
Cheat the Moon	Alcohol	Patricia Hermes
Hannah In Between	Alcohol	Rodowsky
Imitate the Tiger	Alcohol	Jan Cheripko

Wise Highs How to Thrill, Chill, & Get Away from It All Without Alcohol or Other Drugs	Alcohol	Alex J. Packer, Ph.D.
Dynamite Emotions	Anger Management	Kathryn Pearson, M.S.
How to Take the Grrrr out of Anger (8-13 year olds)	Anger Management	Elizabeth Verdick, Marjorie Lisovskis
MAD How to deal with your anger and get respect	Anger Management	James J Crist
I'm Not Bad, I'm Just Mad: A Workbook to Help Kids Control Their Anger	Anger Management	Lawrence E. Shapiro, Zach Pelta-Heller, Anna F. Greenwald
The Bipolar Workbook for Teens	Bipolar	Sheri Van Dijk
Welcome to the Jungle: Everything You Wanted to Know about Bipolar but Were Too Freaked Out to Ask	Bipolar	Hilary Smith
The Childhood Bipolar Disorder Answer Book	Bipolar	Tracy Anglada and Sheryl M. Hakala
Call Me Anna	Bipolar	Patty Duke
Detour: My Bipolar Road Trip in 4-D	Bipolar	Lizzie Simon (Atria Books,2002)
Mind Race: A Firsthand Account of One Teenager's Experience With Bipolar Disorder	Bipolar	Patrick E. Jamieson, PH.D. With Moira A. Rynn, M.D.
My Bipolar Roller Coaster Feeling Book (Elementary ages)	Bipolar	Bryna Hebert
The Ride	Bipolar	M.G. Davis
The Storm in My Brain	Bipolar	
Turbo Max: A Story for Siblings of Children with Bipolar Disorder (8-12 years old)	Bipolar	Tracy Anglada
Matt The Moody Hermit Crab (Grades 4-7)	Bipolar	Caroline C. McGee (McGee & Woods, Inc. 2002)
Everything you need to know about bipolar disorder and manic depressive illness	Bipolar	Michael A Sommers
Brandon and the Bipolar Bear (4-11 year olds)	Bipolar	Tracy Anglada

Tulip Touch	Child Abuse	Anne Fine
Depression is the Pits, but I'm Getting Better	Depression	E. Jane Garland
My Kind of Sad: What It's Like to Be Young and Depressed	Depression	Kate Scowen
Sad Days, Glad Days (a storybook for children about adult depression)	Depression	DeWitt Hamilton
When Nothing Matters Anymore: A Survival Guide for Depressed Teens	Depression	Bev Cobain
Recovering from Depression: A Workbook for Teens	Depression	Mary Ellen Copeland and Stuart Copans
Beyond the Blues: A Workbook to Help Teens Overcome Depression	Depression	Lisa M. Schab
Beauty Queen	Drugs	Linda Glovach
Go Ask Alice	Drugs	Anonymous
Best Little Girl in the World	Eating Disorder	Steven Levenkron
Dying to Be Thin	Eating Disorder	Ira M. Sacker, Marc A. Zimmer
When the Mirror Lies: Anorexia, Bulimia, and Other Eating Disorders	Eating Disorder	Tamra B. Orr
Next to Nothing	Eating Disorder	Carrie Arnold
Picture Perfect: What You Need to Feel Better About Your Body	Eating Disorder	Jill S. Zimmerman Rutledge
What's Eating You?: A Workbook for Teens with Anorexia, Bulimia, and other Eating Disorders	Eating Disorder	Tammy Nelson
Door Near Here - teen	Family Crisis	Heather Quarles
Staying out of Trouble in a Troubled Family	Family Crisis	Rose J. Blue, Corine J. Naden
Stop Pretending: What Happened When My Big Sister Went Crazy	Family Crisis	Sonya Sones
What Do you Really Want?	Goal setting	Beverly Bachel
What do you stand for? For teens	Goal setting	Barbara Lewis
Death Be Not Proud	Grief	John J Gunther
A Teen's Simple Guide to Grief	Grief	Alexis Cunningham

After You Lose Someone You Love	Grief	Amy, Allie, and David Dennison
Forever Hellos, Hard Good-Byes	Grief	Axel Dahlberg and Janis Russell Love
Every Day Counts: Lessons in Love, Faith, and Resilience from Children Facing Illness	Grief	Maria Sirois
Healing Your Grieving Heart for Teens: 100 Practical Ideas	Grief	Alan D. Wolfelt, PH. D
Healing Your Grieving Heart Journal for Teens	Grief	Alan D. Wolfelt, PH. D
I Want to Live	Grief	Lurlene McDaniel
I will Remember You: What to Do When Someone You Love Dies	Grief	Laura Dower
Six Months To Live	Grief	Lurlene McDaniel
Tears of A Tiger	Grief	Sharon Mills Draper
When a Friend Dies: A book for Teens about Grieving and Healing	Grief	Marilyn Gootman
When Will I Stop Hurting? Teens Loss and Grief	Grief	Edward Myers
Young People and Chronic Illness: True Stories, Help and Hope	Grief	Kelly Huegel
The Hero Project: How We Met Our Greatest Heroes and What We Learned from Them	Inspiration	Robert Hatch, William Hatch
Chicken Soup for The Teenage Soul (I, II, III, IV, On tough stuff)	Inspiration	Jack Canfield
Making Every Day Count: Daily Readings for Young People on Solving Problems, Setting Goals and Feeling Good about Yourself	Inspiration	Pamela Espeland, Elizabeth Verdick
Making the Most of Today: Daily Readings for Young People on Self-Awareness, Creativity and Self-Esteem	Inspiration	Pamela Espeland and Rosemary Wallner
Succeed Every Day: Daily Readings for Teens	Inspiration	Pamela Espeland
Clinical Depression and Bipolar Illness: Frequently Asked questions, a Handbook for Teens	Mental Illness	Sallie P. Mink

Dancing on the Edge	Mental Illness	Han Nolan
Embracing the Monster: Overcoming the Challenges of Hidden Disabilities	Mental Illness	Veronica Crawford (Editor)
Humming Whispers	Mental Illness	Angela Johnson
I Can Hear the Mourning Dove	Mental Illness	James W. Bennett
I Never Promised you a Rose Garden	Mental Illness	Joanne Greenberg
It's Kind of a Funny Story	Mental Illness	Ned Vizzini
Language of Goldfish	Mental Illness	Zibby Oneal
Lisa, Bright and Dark	Mental Illness	John Neufeld
Me Nobody Knew: A Story of Triumph for all Girls	Mental Illness	Shannon McLinden
Quiet Room: A Journey out of the Torment of Madness	Mental Illness	Lori Schiller, Amanda Bennett
Sybil	Mental illness	Flora Rheta, Rhea Schreiber
The Bell Jar	Mental illness	Sylvia Plath
Understanding Mental Illness: For Teens Who Care About Someone With Mental Illness	Mental Illness	Julie Tallard Johnson
Behind Happy Faces: Taking Charge of Your Mental Health - A Guide for Young Adults	Mental Illness	Ross Szabo and Melanie Hall
The ADHD Workbook for Teens	Mental Illness	Lara Honos-Webb
Free from OCD: A Workbook for Teens with Obsessive-Compulsive Disorder	OCD	Timothy Sisemore
Kissing Doorknobs	OCD	Terry Spencer Hesser, A. J. Allen
Perfectionism: What's Bad about being too good?	Perfectionism	Miriam Adderholdt and Jan Goldberg
What to Do When Good Enough Isn't Good Enough: The Real Deal on Perfectionism: A Guide for Kids	Perfectionism	Thomas S. Greenspon, Ph.D.
Cut	Self-injury	Patricia McCormick
Stopping the Pain	Self-injury	Lawrence E. Shapiro
Luckiest Girl in The World	Self-injury	Steven Levenkron

I Know why the Caged Bird Sings	Sexual Abuse	Maya Angelou
Incest: Why am I afraid to tell?	Sexual Abuse	Kate Havelin
The Courage to Heal	Sexual Abuse	Ellen Bass and Laura Davis
The Courage to Heal Workbook	Sexual Abuse	Laura Davis
It Happened to Nancy: A True Story from the Diary of A Teenager	Sexual Assault	Beatrice Sparks
GLBTQ: The Survival Guide for Queer and Questioning Teens	Sexual Orientation	Kelly Huegel
Be the Boss of your Stress	Stress	Timothy Culbert and Rebecca Kajander
Cool Cats, Calm Kids: Relaxation and Stress Management for Young People (7-12 years old)	Stress	Mary L. Williams,
Don't Sweat the Small Stuff for Teens: Simple Ways to Keep Your Cool in Stressful Times	Stress	Richard Carlson
The Anxiety Workbook for Teens: Activities to Help You Deal with Anxiety & Worry	Stress	Lisa M. Schab
Fighting Invisible Tigers: A Stress Management Guide for Teens	Stress	Earl Hipp, Pamela Espeland
Stress Can Really Get on Your Nerves! (10-13 years old)	Stress	Trevor Romain, Elizabeth Verdick
Too Stressed to Think?		
A Teen Guide to Staying Sane When Life Makes You Crazy	Stress	Annie Fox, M.Ed., and Ruth Kirschner
What to Do when You Worry Too Much: A Kid's Guide to Overcoming Anxiety (6-12 years old)	Stress	Dawn Huebner
Impulse	Suicide	Ellen Hopkins
Power to Prevent Suicide: A guide for Teens Helping Teens	Suicide	Richard E. Nelson, Judith C. Galas, Pamela Espeland, Bev Cobain
When Happily Ever After Ends	Suicide	Lurlene McDaniel
Coping with Cliques	Teen Coping	Susan Sprague

The Affirmation Weaver and other titles (9-12)	Teen Coping	Lori Lite
The Behavior Survival Guide for Kids: How to Make Good Choices and Stay Out of Trouble	Teen Coping	Thomas McIntyre
Be the Boss of your Pain	Teen Coping	Timothy Culbert and Rebecca Kajander
Be the Boss of your Sleep	Teen Coping	Timothy Culbert and Rebecca Kajander
Bringing Up Parents The Teenager's Handbook	Teen Coping	Alex J. Packer, Ph.D.
Daily Life Strategies for Teens	Teen Coping	Jay McGraw
Growing up Feeling Good: A Growing UP Handbook Especially for Kids	Teen Coping	Ellen Rosenberg
Teenage Body Book	Teen Coping	Kathy McCoy, Charles Wibbelsman
Life Lists for Teens: Tips, Steps, Hints, and How-tos for Growing up, Getting along, Learning, and Having Fun	Teen Coping	Pamela Espeland
The Divorce Workbook for Teens : Activities to Help You Move Beyond the Break Up	Teen Coping	Lisa M. Schab
Life Strategies for Teens Workbook	Teen Coping	Jay McGraw
Life Strategies for Teens	Teen Coping	Jay McGraw
Respect – a girl's guide to Getting Respect and Dealing when your line is crossed	Teen Coping	Courtney Macavinta and Andrea Vander Pluym
See Jane Win for Girls: A Smart Girl's Guide to Success	Teen Coping	Dr. Sylvia Rimm
Stick Up for Yourself	Teen Coping	Gershen Kaufman, Lev Raphael, and Pamela Espeland
The 6 Most Important Decisions You'll Ever Make: A Guide for Teens	Teen Coping	Sean Covey
The Courage to be yourself	Teen Coping	Al Desetta
The Right Moves to Getting Fit and Feeling Great - Girls	Teen Coping	Tina Schwager and Michele Schuerger

The Struggle to be strong	Teen Coping	Al Desetta and Sybil Wolin
Through My Eyes – a journal for teens	Teen Coping	Linda Kranz
What Color Is Your Parachute?: For Teens	Teen Coping	Richard Nelson Bolles, Carol Christen, Jean M. Blomquist
What teens need to succeed : Proven, Practical Ways to Shape Your Own Future	Teen Coping	Peter L Benson, Judy Galbraith, and Pamela Espeland

Depression

Rescuing Your Teenager from Depression by Norman T. Berlinger

Adolescent depression: a guide for parents by Francis Mark Mondimore

The Disappearing Girl: Learning the Language of Teenage Depression by Lisa Machoian

Teens in Turmoil: A Path to Change for Parents, Adolescents, and Their Families by Carol Maxym, Leslie York

If Your Adolescent Has Depression or Bipolar Disorder: An Essential Resource for Parents by Dwight L. Evans, Linda Wasmer Andrews

More than Moody: Recognizing and Treating Adolescent Depression by Harold S. Koplewicz

Help Me, I'm Sad: Recognizing, Treating and Preventing Childhood and Adolescent Depression by David G. Fassler, Lynne S. Dumas

Living Well With Depression and Bipolar Disorder by John McManamy (Collins, 2006)

Straight Talk about Psychiatric Medications for Kids by Timothy E. Wilens, MD (Guilford Press, 2004)

How You Can Survive When They're Depressed: Living and Coping With Depression Fallout by Anne Sheffield PhD

Child and Adolescent Psychopharmacology by Stanley Kutcher, MD

Stability by Mary Ellen Copeland

A Mood Apart by Peter Whybrow, MD

Undoing Depression: What Therapy Doesn't Teach You and Medication Can't Give You by Richard O'Connor PhD

The Omega-3 Connection by Andrew L Stoll

***Out of the Shadows: Confronting America's Mental Illness Crisis by E. Fuller Torrey

When you Worry about the Child you Love: Emotional and Learning Problems in Children by Edward Hallowell

Talking to Depression: Simple Ways to Connect with Someone in your life is Depressed by Claudia J Strauss

I am Not Sick, I Don't Need Help! by Xavier Amador and Anna-Lisa Johanson

Advocating for Someone with a Mental Illness by Sonya Nesch

<u>Overcoming Depression</u> by Demitri Papolos, MD and Janice Papolos

<u>Helping Your Depressed Teenager - A Guide for Parents & Caregivers</u> by Gerald D. Oster, PhD & Sarah S. Montgomery, MSW

<u>Helping Your Depressed Child - A Reassuring Guide to the Causes & Treatments of Childhood & Adolescent Depression</u> by Lawrence L. Kearns, MD

<u>It's Nobody's Fault - New Hope and Help for Difficult Children and Their Parents</u> by Harold S. Koplewicz, MD

<u>Depression in the Young – What We Can Do to Help Them</u> by Trudy Carlson

<u>Depression - Challenge the Beast Within Yourself and Win</u> by Cait Irwin

<u>Helping Your Teenager Beat Depression: A Problem-Solving Approach for Families</u> by Katharina Manassis, Anne Marie Levac, Anne Marie Levac

<u>Monochrome Days: A First-Hand Account of One Teenager's Experience with Depression</u> by Cait Irwin, Dwight L. Evans, Linda Wasmer Andrews

<u>Understanding Teenage Depression: A Guide to Diagnosis, Treatment, and Management</u> by Maureen Empfield, Nicholas Bakalar

<u>Beating Depression: Teens find light at the end of the tunnel</u> by Franklin Watts (Editor), Joan E. Huebl

<u>Coping with Depression in Young People: A Guide for Parents</u> by Carol Fitzpatrick, John Sharry

<u>Helping Your Child Cope with Depression and Suicidal Thoughts</u> by Tonia K. Shamoo, Philip G. Patros

<u>How to Talk So Teens Will Listen & Listen So Teens Will Talk</u> by Adele Faber, Elaine Mazlish

<u>The Depression Workbook: A Guide for Living With Depression and Manic Depression</u> by Mary Ellen Copeland

<u>Overcoming Teen Depression: A Guide for Parents</u> by Miriam Kaufman

<u>Mental Health Information for Teens</u> by Karen Bellenir

<u>The Teen Brain Book: Who and What Are You</u> by Dale Bick Carlson & Nancy Teasdale

Bipolar

The Bipolar Child by Demitri F. Papolos, MD & Janice Papolos

Bipolar Teen: What You Can Do to Help Your Child and Your Family by David J. Miklowitz, Elizabeth L. George

The Bipolar Handbook for Teens and Kids by Wes Burgess

Parenting a Bipolar Child: What to Do & Why by Gianni L. Faedda and Nancy B. Austin

What Works for Bipolar Kids: Help and Hope for Parents by Mani Pavuluri and Susan

Is Your Child Bipolar?: The Definitive Resource on How to Identify, Treat, and Thrive with a Bipolar Child by Mary Ann Mcdonnell and Janet Wozniak

Understanding the Mind of Your Bipolar Child: The Complete Guide to the Development, Treatment, and Parenting of Children with Bipolar Disorder by Gregory T. Lombardo

Teaching Kids With Mental Health and Learning Disorders in the Regular Classroom: How to Recognize, Understand, and Help Challenged (And Challenging) Students Succeed by Myles L. Cooley

Madness: A Bipolar Life by Marya Hornbacher

Educating and Nurturing the Bipolar Child: The first DVD Focusing on the Educational Issues of Children and Adolescents with Bipolar Disorder by Janice Papolos (produced by the Juvenile Bipolar Research Foundation)

Intense Minds by Tracy Anglada

Parenting a Bipolar Child by Gianni L. Faedda, MD and Nancy B. Austin, PsyD (New Harbinger Publications, Inc., 2006)

New Hope for Children and Teens with Bipolar Disorder: Your Friendly, Authoritative Guide to the Latest in Traditional and Complementary Solutions, (Three Rivers Press, 2004)

Raising a Moody Child: How to Cope with Depression and Bipolar Disorder by Jill S. Goldberg Arnold, MD and Mary A. Fristad, MD (The Guilford Press, 2004)

The Explosive Child by Ross W. Greene, PhD (Harper Collins, 1998)

If Your Child Is Bipolar: The Parent-to-Parent Guide To Living

With and Loving a Bipolar Child by Cindy Singer and Sheryl Gurrentz (Perspective Publishing, 2003)

The Bipolar Disorder Survival Guide: What You and Your Family Need to Know by David J. Miklowitz, PhD (The Guilford Press, 2002)

Bipolar Disorders: A Guide to Helping Children and Adolescents by Mitzi Waltz (O'Reilly, 2000)

Overcoming Bipolar Disorder by Mark S. Bauer, Devra E. Greenwald, Amy M. Kilbourne, Evette J. Ludman

Bipolar 101: A Practical Guide to Identifying Triggers, Managing Medications, Coping with Symptoms, and More by Ruth C. White, John Preston

Living with Bipolar: A Guide to Understanding and Managing the Disorder by Lesley Berk

When Someone You Love Is Bipolar: Help and Support for You and Your Partner by Cynthia G. Last, PhD

Why Am I Still Depressed: Recognizing and Managing the Ups and Downs of Bipolar II and Soft Bipolar Disorder by Jim R. Phelps, MD; foreword by Nassir Ghaemi, MD, MPH

Living in Storms: Contemporary Poetry and the Moods of Manic Depression by Thom Schramm

The Cognitive Behavioral Workbook for Depression: A Step-by-Step Program by William J. Knaus, EdD

Hurry Down Sunshine by Michael Greenberg

Survival Strategies for Parenting Children with Bipolar Disorder by George T. Lynn (Jessica Kingsley Publishers, 2001)

His Bright Light by Danielle Steel (Delacorte, 1998)

Acquainted With the Night by Paul Raeburn (Broadway, 2004)

The Life of a Bipolar Child by Trudy Carlson (Benline Press, 1995) (formerly The Suicide of My Son)

Manic Depression and Creativity by D. Jablow Hershman and Julian Lieb Prometheus Books, 1998)

Win the Battle: The 3-Step Lifesaving Formula to Conquer Depression and Bipolar Disorder by Bob Olson (Chandler House Press, 1999)

When Madness Comes Home by Victoria Secunda (Hyperion, 1998)

Get Out of My Life, But First Could You Drive Cheryl and Me to the Mall? by Anthony E. Wolf, PhD (The Noonday Press, 1991)

Surviving Manic-Depression: A Manual on Bipolar Disorder for Patients, Families, and Providers by E. Fuller Torrey and Michael B. Knable (Basic Books, 2002)

The Price of Greatness: Resolving the Creativity and Madness Controversy by Arnold Ludwig

Bipolar Disorder: A Guide for Patients and Families by Francis Mark Mondimore

Living Without Depression and Manic Depression: A workbook for Maintaining Moodswing by Ronald Fieve, MD

New Hope for People with Bipolar Disorder by Jan Fawcett

Touched with Fire: Manic depressive Illness and the Artistic Temperament by Kay Redfield Jamison

Uniquely Gifted: Identifying and Meeting the Needs of the Twice Exceptional Student by Kiesa Kay

The Ups and Downs of Raising A Bipolar Child by Judith Lederman and Candida Fink

What Goes up... Surviving the Manic Episode of a Loved One by Judy Eron

Imagining Robert: My Brother, Madness and Survival by Jay Neugeboren

The Bipolar Workbook: Tools for Controlling Your Mood Swings by Monica Ramirez Basco

New Hope for Children and Teens with Bipolar Disorder: Your Friendly, Authoritative Guide to the Latest in Traditional and Complementary Solutions by Boris Birmaher

Living Without Depression and Manic Depression: A Workbook for Maintaining Mood Stability by Mary Ellen Copeland

Loving Someone With Bipolar Disorder by Julie A. Fast, John D.Preston

Bipolar Disorder for Dummies by Candida Fink, MD, and Joe Kraynak

Manic-Depressive Illness: Bipolar Disorders and Recurrent Depression by Frederick K. Goodwin and Kay Redfield Jamison

Bipolar Kids: Helping Your Child Find Calm in the Mood Storm by Rosalie Greenberg, MD

To Walk on Eggshells by Jean Johnston
Bipolar and the Art of Roller-coaster Riding by Madeleine Kelly
Dancing with Bipolar Bears: Living in Joy Despite Illness by James E McReynolds
Friends and Family Bipolar Survival Guide by Debra and Mark Meehl
The Bipolar Disorder Survival Guide: What You and Your Family Need to Know by David J. Miklowitz
Why Am I Still Depressed: Recognizing and Managing the Ups and Downs of Bipolar II and Soft Bipolar Disorder by Jim Phelps, MD
Acquainted With the Night: A Parent's Quest to Understand Depression and Bipolar Disorder in His Children by Paul Raeburn
The Normal One: Life with a Difficult or Damaged Sibling by Jeanne Safer, PhD
Mad House: Growing Up in the Shadow of Mentally Ill Siblings by Clea Simon
If Your Child is Bipolar: The Parent-to-Parent Guide to Living with and Loving a Bipolar Child by Cindy Singer and Sheryl Gurrentz
Bipolar Disorders: A Guide to Helping Children and Adolescents by Mitzi Walsh
Bipolar Survival Guide by, David Markowitz, MD
Loving Someone with Bipolar Disorder by Julie A. Fast and John D. Preston
I Hate You-Don't Leave Me: Understanding the Borderline Personality by Jerold J. Kriesman MD, Hal Straus
Finding Your Bipolar Muse: How to Master Depressive Droughts and Manic Floods and Access Your Creative Power by Lana R. Castle
Kids in the Syndrome Mix of ADHD, LD, Asperger's, Tourette's, Bipolar and More!: The One Stop Guide for Parents, Teachers and Other Professionals by Martin L., MD Kutscher, Robert R. Wolff, and Tony Attwood
Bipolar Disorder in Childhood and Early Adolescence by Barbara Geler and Melissa P Delbello

Substance Abuse
90 Ways to Keep Your Kids Drug Free by Karen Milici Palmiero
Preventing Addiction: What Parents Must Know to Immunize Their Kids against Drug and Alcohol Addiction by John C. Fleming
Drug and Alcohol Abuse: The Authoritative Guide for Parents, Teachers, and Counselors by H. Thomas Milhorn
Drugproof Kids: The Ultimate Prevention Handbook for Parents to Protect Children from Addictions by Frank Jr Simonelli
Just Say Know: Talking with Kids about Drugs and Alcohol by Cynthia Kuhn, Scott Swartzwelder, Wilkie Wilson, Scott Swartzwelder, Wilkie Wilson
Saying No Is Not Enough - Helping Your Kids Make Wise Decisions About Alcohol, Tobacco, and Other Drugs (2nd Edition) by Robert Schwebel, Benjamin Spock
Raising Drug-Free Kids: 100 Tips for Parents by Aletha J. Solter
Big Book Unplugged: A Young Person's Guide to Alcoholics Anonymous by John Rosengren, Anonymous
Young, Sober and Free: Teen-to-Teen Stories of Hope and Recovery by Shelly Marshall
Teens Under the Influence: The Truth About Kids, Alcohol, and Other Drugs - How to Recognize the Problem and What to Do About It by Katherine Ketcham, Nicholas A. Pace, Nicholas A. Pace
Teen Addiction by Jill Karson
Adolescent Substance Abuse Treatment in the United States: Exemplary Models from a National Evaluation Study by Sally J. Stevens, Andrew R. Morral
Adolescent Substance Abuse: New Frontiers in Assessment by Ken C. Winters (Editor)
Smashed: Story of a Drunken Girlhood by Koren Zailckas

Suicide/Self Injury
Dying to Be Free: A Healing Guide for Families after a Suicide by Beverly Cobain, Jean Larch
Bodily Harm: The Breakthrough Treatment Program for Self-Injurers by Karen Conterio, Wendy Lader, PhD with Jennifer

Bloom

Night Falls Fast: Understanding Suicide by Kay Redfield Jamison

Take the Dimness of My Soul Away: Healing after a Loved One's Suicide by William A. Ritter

Finding Your Way after the Suicide of Someone You Love by David B. Biebel, Suzanne L. Foster

How I Stayed Alive When My Brain Was Trying to Kill Me: One Person's Guide to Suicide Prevention by Susan Rose Blauner

Suicide: The Forever Decision: For Those Thinking about Suicide, and for Those Who Know, Love, and Counsel Them by Paul G. Quinnett

When Living Hurts: For Teenagers, Young Adults, Their Parents, Leaders, and Counselors by Sol Gordon

No One Saw My Pain - Why Teens Kill Themselves by Andrew Slaby, MD & Lili Frank Garfinkel

Will's Choice: A Suicidal Teen, a Desperate Mother, and a Chronicle of Recovery by Gail Griffith

Eating Disorders

Parent's Guide to Eating Disorders: Supporting Self-Esteem, Healthy Eating, and Positive Body Image at Home by Marcia Herrin, Nancy Matsumoto

Treating Bulimia in Adolescents: A Family-Based Approach by Danielle Grange, James Lock

If Your Adolescent Has an Eating Disorder : An Essential Resource for Parents by B. Timothy Walsh, V. L. Cameron

Understanding Weight and Depression by Julie M. Clarke, Ann Kirby-Payne

Grief

Grieving: A Beginner's Guide by Jerusha Hall Hull McCormack

Life After Loss by Bob Deits

Your Healing Journey Through Grief by Stanley Cornlis

The Grieving Child: A Parent's Guide by Helen Fitzgerald

Child Survivors of Suicide: A Guidebook for Those Who Care for Them by Rebecca Parkin with Karen Dunne-Maxim

Helping Children Grieve by Theresa Huntley

Helping Children Cope with the loss of a loved one by William C. Kroen
Bereaved Children and Teens by Earl A Grollman
Helping Teens Cope with Death by the Dougy Center

Web Resources and Hotlines

General Mental Illness

National Alliance of the Mentally Ill (NAMI) http://www.nami.org/ 1-800-950-NAMI
Mental Health America www.nmha.org 800-969-6642
National Institute for Mental Health
    http://www.nimh.nih.gov/ 800-421-4211
Depression and Bipolar Support Alliance (DBSA) www.dbsalliance.org 800-826-3632
Bring Change 2 Mind To fight the stigma of mental illness http://www.bringchange2mind.org/
The International Mental Health Research Organization (IMHRO) supports research on mental health http://www.imhro.org/
Minds on the edge http://www.mindsontheedge.org/ is a website to support a PBS special with the same name that explores mental illness and encourages people to talk about it.
NARSAD funds brain and behavior research. http://www.narsad.org/
Unveiling the Stigma is passionate about helping to combat the stigma of mental illness. http://www.unveilingthestigma.com/
The National Mental health Awareness Campaign www.nostigma.org
Special Education Law www.wrightslaw.com
The Bazelon Center for Mental Health Law www.bazelon.org
American Psychiatric Association www.healthyminds.org
1800 Therapist for help finding one www.1-800-therapist.com
Medicaid Resources www.nasmd.org/links/state_medicaid_links.asp

Screening for Mental Health www.mentalhealthscreening.org
Depression Central http://www.psycom.net/depression.central.html
SAMHSA – National Mental Health Information Center http://mentalhealth.samhsa.gov/   (800) 789-2647
The Carter Center's Mental Health Program http://www.cartercenter.org/health/mental_health/index.html
Anxiety disorders http://www.freedomfromfear.org/index.asp

Teen/Child Mental Illness

Teen/child mental illness
Child and Adolescent Bipolar Foundation www.Bpkids.org 877-927-5437
Teenscreen Program www.teenscreen.org
Teen focused web site http://www.bpkids.org/flipswitch
Pendulum Resources http://www.pendulum.org/
Juvenile Bipolar Research Foundation 866-333-JBRF www.jbrf.org
The Bipolar Child www.bipolarchild.com
Girls Health http://www.girlshealth.gov/
Cope Care Deal www.copecaredeal.org A mental health site for teens
Families for Depression Awareness www.familyaware.org
AACAP (American Academy of Child and Adolescent Psychiatry) http://www.aacap.org/
Federation of Families for Children's Mental Health http://www.ffcmh.org/
The National Center for Juvenile Justice and Mental Health http://www.ncmhjj.com
United Parents for Families in Crisis http://www.unitedparents.org/
Jed Foundation - The Jed Foundation is the nation's leading organization working to prevent suicide and promote mental health among college students http://www.jedfoundation.org/
Live Strong http://www.livestrong.com/ Guides to balance, exercise and health

Family Guide To Keeping Youth Mentally Healthy and Drug Free http://www.family.samhsa.gov A public education Web site, developed to support the efforts of parents and other caring adults to promote mental health and prevent the use of alcohol, tobacco, and illegal drugs among 7- to 18-year-olds.

Focus Adolescent Services http://www.focusas.com/ An Internet clearinghouse offering resources, support, and information to help parents and families navigate the troubled waters of adolescence.

Active Minds Working to change the conversation about mental illness on college campuses http://www.activeminds.org/index. php

Active Minds on Campus www.activemindsoncampus.org

NAMI's Youth Networking site www.strengthofus.org

Jed Foundation College Focused site www.halfofus.org

Videos for teens on depression

http://www.morethansad.org/indextd.html

http://us.reachout.com/wecanhelpus/index.php

The Federation of Families for Children's Mental Health www. ffcmh.org

---

Helping Children Cope After A Disaster

http://childadvocate.net/help_children_cope.htm
A printable booklet developed by the Penn State University Pediatric Trauma team to help parents and professionals deal with disaster and related issues.

After the Disaster: A Children's Mental Health Checklist ▰▰▱
http://www.fema.gov/kids/tch_mntl.htm A checklist to assess a child's mental health status, following a disaster or traumatic experience.

Internet Special Education Resources http://www.iser.com/ This is a nationwide directory of professionals serving learning disabled and special education communities.

Safer Child, Inc. http://www.saferchild.org/drugs&.htm Safer Child, Inc. provides parents, caregivers, and educators worldwide with the resources and information to help all children grow up healthy, safe and happy. The group addresses topics such as mental health, substance abuse, and violence.

4girls.gov http://www.4girls.gov
Sponsored by the Office on Women's Health in the Department of Health and Human Services, gives girls information that will help them to understand their health needs right now and as they grow into women. This site is designed especially for girls between the ages of 14 and 19, and provides reliable, current health information that focuses on the many health topics pertaining to adolescent girls' health concerns.

www.Bam.gov BAM! Body and Mind is an online destination for kids created by the Centers for Disease Control and Prevention (CDC). Designed for kids 9-13 years old, BAM! Body and Mind gives them the information they need to make healthy lifestyle choices.

Suicide

American Association of Suicidology www.suicidology.org
Suicide Preventions, Awareness and Support www.Suicide.org
Self injury www.selfinjury.com
Suicide Awareness Voices of Education http://www.save.org/
SAVE's Mission is to prevent suicide through public awareness and education, eliminate stigma and serve as a resource to those touched by suicide.
Suicide Prevention Action Network (SPAN USA)
http://www.spanusa.org/ SPAN is dedicated to preventing suicide through public education and awareness, community action and federal, state and local grassroots advocacy.
The American Foundation for Suicide Prevention (AFSP)
http://www.afsp.org/ AFSP is the only national not-for-profit organization exclusively dedicated to understanding and preventing suicide through research and education, and to reaching out to people with mood disorders and those affected by suicide.

Suicide Hotline lists: http://suicidehotlines.com/

1-800 SUICIDE (1-800-784-2433) http://www.hopeline.com/
National Hopeline: 1-800-442-HOPE (4673)
National Suicide Prevention lifeline
1-800-273-TALK (8255)   http://www.suicidepreventionlifeline.
org/
24 hours a day, 7 days a week
Karla Smith Foundation was founded to honor a 26 year old suicide victim and provide support and information for family and friends with mental illness and those with suicidal ideation. http://www.karlasmithfoundation.org

Alcohol/Substance Abuse/Smoking

Al-Anon/Al-Ateen http://www.al-anon.org/alateen.html
1-888 4 AL-ANON – Alcoholic in the family
(888-425-2666)   8am - 6pm EST, Monday - Friday

Alcoholics Anonymous http://www.alcoholics-anonymous.org

Narcotics Anonymous www.na.org

Center for Substance Abuse Treatment Referral Helpline
1-800 662 HELP (800 662 4357)   24 hours a day, 7 days a week

National Clearinghouse for Drug and Alcohol Information
800-729-6686 http://ncadi.samhsa.gov/

Partnership for a Drugfree America http://www.drugfree.org/
Girl Scouts of America – "In the Zone" drug prevention workbook   800-221-6707
National Institute on Drug Abuse http://www.teens.drugabuse.
gov/
Info on Drugs and teens: www.abovetheinfluence.com
Office of National Drug Control Policy www.
whitehousedrugpolicy.gov
Parental information on drugs www.theantidrug.com

Treating Teens: A guide to Adolescent Drug Programs
http://www.drugstrategies.org/teens/index.html

Office on Smoking and Health (CDC) 770-488-5705 www.cdc.gov/tobacco
American Cancer Society 800-ACS-2345 www.cancer.org
American Lung Association 800-586-4872 www.lungusa.org
Nicotine Anonymous 415-750-0328 www.nicotine-anonymous.org
www.thetruth.com

Sexual Assault / Domestic Abuse/Violence

National Sexual Assault Hotline   1-800 656 4673
24 hours a day, 7 days a week
National Domestic Violence Hotline 1-800 799 SAFE (800 799 7233)
24 hours a day, 7 days a week   www.ndvh.org
National Teen Dating Abuse Helpline 1-866-331-9474,
http://loveisrespect.org/
Childhelp USA (Child Abuse hotline) 1-800-422-4453
http://www.childhelp.org/
National Youth Violence Prevention Resource Center
http://www.safeyouth.org/scripts/teens.asp
1-866-SAFE YOUTH (723-3968)
Parents Anonymous – Child abuse prevention
www.parentsanonymous.org
National Coalition against Domestic Violence
http://www.ncadv.org/

Teen Sexual Orientation

---

http://www.youthresource.com/ - Web site created by and for gay, lesbian, bisexual, transgender, and questioning (GLBTQ) young people 13 to 24 years

Crisis Intervention/suicide prevention for Gay Youth *"Trevor Helpline"*
1-866 4 U TREVOR (866 488 7386) http://www.thetrevorproject.org/
24 hours a day, 7 days a week

The Gay & Lesbian National Help Center http://www.glnh.org/index2.html
1-888 THE GLNH (888 843 4564)
Youth talkline: 1-800- 246–PRIDE (7743)
Parents and Friends of Gays and Lesbians http://www.pflag.org/
National Youth Advocacy Coalition www.nyacyouth.org
Gay-Straight Alliance Network www.gsanetwork.org
 Empowering youth activists to fight homophobia and transphobia in schools.
The National Coalition for Gay, Lesbian, Bisexual & Transgender Youth http://www.outproud.org/
Gay, Lesbian and Straight Education Network www.glsen.org
For Transgender Youth http://imatyfa.org

Eating Disorders

National Eating Disorders Association http://www.nationaleatingdisorders.org/ 1-800-931-2237
National Association of Anorexia and Associated Disorders 1-847-831-3438 www.anad.org
Sheena's Place http://www.sheenasplace.org/
Kids and Eating Disorders
http://www.kidshealth.org/kid/health_problems/learning_problem/eatdisorder.html
This site is intended for use by kids and provides information on body image and eating disorders
Academy for eating disorders http://www.aedweb.org/
The Academy for Eating Disorders is an international transdisciplinary professional organization that promotes

excellence in research, treatment and prevention of eating disorders. The AED provides education, training and a forum for collaboration and professional dialogue.

Grief

The Dougy Center http://www.dougy.org/ - a safe place for children, teens, young adults and families to grieve.
GriefShare www.griefrecovery.com - a friendly, caring group of people who will walk alongside you through one of life's most difficult experiences.

General hotlines for advice

Kids, Need to Talk?
Are you or a friend looking for answers to tough questions?
Covenant House Nineline can help. Call our hotline to talk about your concerns. Anywhere. Anytime. 1-800-999-9999. It's free, it's confidential, it's 24/7 and it's for you! http://www.nineline.org/index.html/

http://www.teenlineonline.org/If you have a problem - any kind of problem - and you want to talk with another teen, *someone who understands,* then this is the right place for you ... **Teen Line is a hotline operated *by* teens, *for* teens** . 310-855-HOPE (4673) 6pm to 10pm PST (California time) every night
http://www.sexetc.org/ A web site for teens by teens about Girls' Health, Guys' Health, Sex, Love & Relationships, sexual orientation, Pregnancy, Emotional Health, Abuse & Violence, and Body Image

Bibliography

AACAP. (n.d.). Retrieved from http://www.aacap.org/cs/root/facts_for_families/teen_suicide

CAREY, B. (2007, Sept. 7). Retrieved 1 24, 2009, from http://query.nytimes.com/gst/fullpage.html?res=9906E7DB143AF934A3575AC0A9619C8B63

Child and Adolescent Bipolar Foundation. (n.d.). Retrieved from Child and Adolescent Bipolar Foundation: http://www.bpkids.org/site/PageServer?pagename=lrn_about

Christine T. Finn, M. (n.d.). *A Brief Overview of the Genetics of Bipolar Disorder.* Retrieved from http://focus.psychiatryonline.org/cgi/content/full/5/1/14

Finegold, P. (n.d.). *The Biological Basis of Mental Illness.* Retrieved from http://www.geneticfutures.com/cracked/info/sheet9.asp

Flaherty, A. (2004). *The Midnight Disease: The Drive to Write, Writer's Block, and the Creative Brain.* Houghton Mifflin Harcourt.

Isabelle M Rosso, C. M.-T. (Vol. 57, No. 1. (1 January 2005)). Amygdala and hippocampus volumes in pediatric major depression. *Biological Psychiatry* , 21-26.

Jamison, K. R. (1994). *Touched with Fire.* Simon and Schuster.

Psychiatric Disorders. (Dec, 16 2008). Retrieved from http://www.psychiatric-disorders.com/articles/bipolar-disorder/bp-children.php

Raymond Lemberg, L. C. (1999). *Eating Disorders.* Greenwood Publishing Group.

Shaffer, D. G. (1996). Psychiatric diagnosis in child and adolescent suicide. *Archives of General Psychiatry* , 53; 339-348.

Spangler, D. (1998). *Parent as Mystic, Mystic as Parent.* Riverhead Books.

What percentage of individuals with severe psychiatric disorders are receiving no treatment? (2007, April). Retrieved from www.treatmentadvocacycenter.org

Important disclaimers about medications

This is the fine print about medications required by the FDA that no one ever reads, but is really important.

1) Antidepressant medicine may increase suicidal thoughts or actions in some children, teenagers, and young adults when the medicine is first started.

2) Depression and other serious mental illnesses are the most important causes of suicidal thoughts and actions. Some people may have a particularly high risk of having suicidal thoughts or actions. These include people who have (or have a family history of) bipolar illness or suicidal thoughts or actions.

3) How can I watch for and try to prevent suicidal thought and actions in myself and family members?
   a) Pay close attention to any changes, especially sudden, in mood, behaviors, or feelings. This is very important when an antidepressant is first started or when the dose is changed.
   b) Call the healthcare provider right away to report new or sudden changes in mood, behavior, thoughts or feelings.
   c) Keep all follow-up visits with the healthcare provider as scheduled. Call the healthcare provider between visits as needed, especially if you have concerns about symptoms.

4) **Never** stop an antidepressant without first talking to a healthcare provider. That may cause other symptoms.
5) Antidepressants can interact with other medications. Tell the healthcare provider about any other medications that you might be taking.

My Contact Information

Name:_____

Address:_____

Phones: Home _____Cell _____

Work _____

Diagnosis: _____

My Parents

Dad(_____)

Phones:

Home_____

Cell_____

Work_____

Mom(_____)

Phones:

Home_____

Cell_____

Work_____

Other:

Phones:

Home_____

Cell_____

Work_____

My Doctors

Primary Care: Name:_____

Address: _____

Phone:_____

Psychiatrist Name:_____

Address: _____

Phone:_____

Therapist Name:_____

Address: _____

Phone:_____

My Preferred Hospital Name:_____

Address: _____

Phone:_____Emergency Room:_____

Other Important Phone Numbers

911

Local Suicide hotline:_____

National Suicide hotline: 1 800-SUICIDE (1-800-784-2433)

Health Insurance

Name:_____

Policy Number: _____Group Number:_____

Phone:_____

Medications I am taking (for all illness)

1>	Dosage
2>	Dosage
3>	Dosage
4>	Dosage

MY PHONE LIST

Local Suicide Hotline_____

National Suicide hotline: 1 800-SUICIDE (1-800-784-2433)

Therapist_____

Psychiatrist_____

Friend_____

Friend_____

Church_____

Emergency 911_____

Pharmacy _____

<u>My Parents</u>

Dad(_____)

Phones:

Home _____

Cell_____

Work_____

Mom(_____)

Phones:

Home_____

Cell_____

Work_____

Others_____

_____

_____

Suicide Contract

I,_____, hereby agree that I will not harm myself in any way, attempt suicide, or die by suicide.

Furthermore, I agree that I will take the following actions if I am ever suicidal:

1) I will remind myself that I can never, under any circumstances, harm myself in any way, attempt suicide, or die by suicide.

2) I will call **911** or **1-800-SUICIDE (800-784-2433)** if I believe that I am in immediate danger of harming myself.

3) I will call any or all of the following numbers if I am not in immediate danger of harming myself but have suicidal thoughts No one will think I am weak or bad for asking for help.

Signed,_____Date:_____

Friends or family to call for help: Phone:

_____

_____

<u>(Make sure you have told these friends about this contract</u> – they might want to read the book: *Power to Prevent Suicide: A Guide for Teens Helping Teens*")

<u>OR</u>

My Doctor:_____Phone:_____

<u>OR</u>

these suicide hotlines

1-800-SUICIDE (800-784-2433)

1-800-273-TALK
1-800-442-HOPE (4673)
Local teen hotline:_____

<u>OR</u>

911